Transforming Social Work Practice – titles in the series

To order, please contact our distributor: BEBC Distribution, Albion Close, Parkstone, Poole, BH12 3LL. Telephone: 0845 230 9000, email: **learningmatters@bebc.co.uk**. You can also find more information on each of these titles and our other learning resources at **www.learningmatters.co.uk**.

New Directions in Social Work Practice

KIERON HATTON

Series Editors: Jonathan Parker and Greta Bradley

LearningMatters

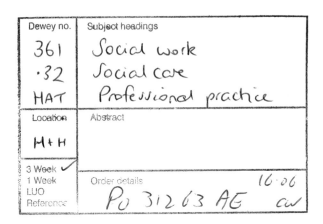
First published in 2008 by Learning Matters Ltd

British Library Cataloguing in Publication Data
A CIP record for this book is available from the British Library.

ISBN 978 1 84445 079 4

Cover and text design by Code 5 Design Associates Ltd
Project management by Deer Park Productions, Tavistock
Typeset by PDQ Typesetting Ltd
Printed and bound in Great Britain by Cromwell Press, Trowbridge, Wiltshire

Learning Matters Ltd
33 Southernhay East
Exeter EX1 1NX
Tel: 01392 215560
info@learningmatters.co.uk
www.learningmatters.co.uk

Contents

Acknowledgements

Thanks to all members of the Centre for Social Work at the University of Portsmouth for their support, inspiration and openness to new ideas. Particular thanks to Pete Shepherd and Kim Brown for reading drafts of the material.

Thanks also to all those colleagues, whether they be academics, social workers/peda-gogues or people who used services, who contributed, directly and indirectly, to the theories and practices underpinning the book. A particular thanks to staff at Frobelse-minariet in Copenhagen and members of the Social Work Inclusion Group at the University. It is to the University of Portsmouth's credit that it is so committed to international, inter-professional and inclusive strategies.

The book is dedicated to Helen, Cal and Ruari without whose support I would never have finished it.

Introduction

If you don't risk anything, you risk more.

Erica Jong

I risk crossing the road because otherwise I risk standing still,
I risk being honest because otherwise I risk never knowing,
I risk being in a relationship because otherwise I risk never learning to care,
I risk eating chocolate because otherwise I risk missing out,
I risk a sense of humour because otherwise I risk going mad,
I risk being misunderstood because otherwise
I risk never being understood at all

Creative Writing Working Party
University of Portsmouth, 2006

Social work is confronting significant challenges at the beginning of the twenty-first century. Despite the development of a newer, more mature professional identity since the introduction of the Care Standards Act 2000, the introduction of a three-year pre-qualifying degree programme, and the processes of regulation and accreditation through the General Social Care Council, social work faces challenges on a number of fronts.

The increased emphasis on partnership working can often seem to leave social work as the junior partner in relationships with big spending professions such as health and education. The workforce below social work qualification level is still poorly qualified and new types of worker are being put forward as potential rivals or alternatives to social work. Service users and carers are articulating their own agendas in ways which question the right of professionals, including social workers, to make decisions about people's lives without full consideration of the voice of these previously ignored or marginalised groups. This book seeks to examine these challenges and pose a set of alternative scenarios for social work which will cement its place in welfare provision but in ways which are accountable, democratic and innovative.

The book will be organised around three key themes.

- **Inclusion** If social work is to make a real impact on the lives of those people who are marginalised and excluded it needs to develop a frame of reference which values, hears and works in partnerships with the people who are experts in social work, those who use social work services.

- **Inter-professionalism** Too often inter-professionalism is seen as an unequal relationship in which the most powerful partner – statutory as against voluntary organisations, health or education as against social work – sets the agenda and structures the way services are developed and delivered. This book suggests a different way in which these partnerships can be framed which enhances the role of social work.

- **Internationalism**   It sometimes appears as if social work sees itself as solely a national activity which is impermeable to international or global influence. This view is being increasingly challenged and if social work is to continue to demonstrate its relevance it needs to listen to and learn from practitioners and theorists in other countries.

Central to these themes is the idea of innovation. If social work is going to grasp the opportunities available to it, it needs to be innovative, creative and critical. New forms of practice are emerging which encompass these emerging themes. However, they are often imperfectly developed, unevenly practised and poorly theorised. This book seeks to explore the dilemmas around these issues, and to suggest, drawing on UK and European examples, ways in which they can be incorporated into new forms of welfare practice.

The notion of creativity is central to this reconfigured social work agenda. The poem which opens this chapter resulted from the collaboration of service users/carers from the Social Work Inclusion Group (SWIG) at the University of Portsmouth with UK and international students in the development of a creative workshop to explore issues of identity, difference and diversity. The agenda for the day was driven by the desire of members of SWIG to explore ways of communicating their feelings, desires and ability to influence the social work agenda in a way which they could control and which reflected their concerns and aspirations. The decision to use creativity to enhance this process was not accidental but was rather the result of SWIG members' frustrations with traditional methods of collaboration and a desire to show that they had the capacity and ability to explore complex issues around their experience without having their views mediated by professionals. The poem powerfully reflects a major concern of service users and carers that current social work practice has become risk averse. This is despite the views expressed in recent policy developments such as *Valuing people; Independence, well-being and choice;* and *Our health, our care, our say* (see Chapters 1 and 5). The safety-first practice of much current social work, reinforced as it is by a managerialist focus on outcomes rather than the social work task (Dominelli and Hoogvelt, 1996; Davis and Garrett, 2004), makes the achievement of such risk enhancing practice even less likely to occur.

A key theme within the book will therefore be to explore the possibilities for a new creative agenda to frame social work practice. As Lymbery (2003) has noted, the competence framework within which current social work operates is not likely to be abandoned. Indeed the work around redefining the key roles and tasks for social work which is at present underway is likely to embed the competence framework even further into current and future practice. The task therefore becomes one of utilising the possibilities that exist to recognise uncertainty and embrace it as a means of understanding the complexity of the social work task. As Lymbery notes, *the application of . . . creativity will be linked to a number of factors: the level of complexity of the work, the degree of familiarity of the practitioner with the type of work, and so on* (Lymbery, 2003,p109). He suggests that in particular creativity is likely to be embraced more by higher-level practitioners, especially at post-qualifying level. He suggests that it is in the areas of assessment and evaluation that the potential for creativity is most likely to be found.

Although we can welcome this attempt to reintroduce creativity into UK social work, the analysis of Lymbery and others suffers from an over-concern with the national context. As noted earlier, social work needs to embrace the lessons of practice in other countries. The work of Cameron, McQuail and Petrie (2007) points to the potential of integrating a European tradition – pedagogy – into the UK. A central element of pedagogic practice concerns the use of creativity to build relationships between pedagogues and the people they work with. Creativity in this context can therefore be seen as part of a process of collaboration and empowerment (see Chapters 6 and 7).

Chambers (2004) suggests that social pedagogy may provide a link to these notions of creativity. As she notes, the use of creativity can be part of a strategy to improve services. Writing specifically about children's health she notes the:

> Interconnection between personal empowerment, increased self-esteem and confidence, personal growth and social inclusion, and enhanced psychological and physical health... participation in arts activities helps people to discover their potential, to release their talents and to raise their self esteem.
>
> (Chambers, 2004, p1)

A similar claim about the potential efficacy of community arts to promote community empowerment is made by Boehm and Boehm (2003).

This book therefore seeks to develop a definition of creativity which encompasses both the desire to improve current practice and new forms of practice. Creativity in this definition can therefore be seen to have three central elements to it.

- To modify existing ways of doing things to make them more relevant to people providing and experiencing services.

- To challenge current ways of doing things and in particular to expose the limitations of forms of practice which focus on outcomes and which neglect relationships as an integral part of practice.

- To develop new ways of doing things which build on the best elements of current practice but which also draw on European traditions of pedagogy and social pedagogy.

The structure of this book

To achieve these goals the book begins by examining policy developments in social work and identifies a number of key characteristics of the wide-ranging legislative timetable which has been introduced since the election of New Labour in 1997. Chapter 1 seeks to delineate the way these new policies have developed and to suggest continuities across policy development in social work, particularly around issues of independence, choice, well-being and partnership. It points out however, how these objectives are also cross-cut with the contradictory policies of regulation and advocacy. Chapter 2 demonstrates how this is not a new dilemma but that it can be traced back to earlier debates around radical social and community development. Chapter 3 looks at the way in which these shared traditions, of radical social and community work, can be used to develop new forms of practice that utilise an agenda which promotes social change.

This in turn raises issues about the role of social work as a professional activity and the way in which social work is developing within a contemporary context. Chapter 4 looks at the importance of the voluntary sector in promoting alternative ways of delivering services. It also points to the way in which debates around communitarianism have led to an attempt to dampen down the radicalism of the sector and the way in which the government has sought to promote those elements of the voluntary sector which concentrate on service delivery rather than oppositional work or an agenda promoting social change.

One area where there does appear to have been a commitment to a more radical agenda, which promotes new forms of practice, is in the emphasis placed on the involvement and participation of people who use services. Chapter 5 demonstrates the wide-ranging nature of this commitment and points to the legislative and policy framework within which these developments have occurred. It draws attention also to the way in which these debates are not only taking place in the UK but are part of a wider European debate about the nature of welfare provision. It suggests that involvement has to mean a tangible rather than tokenistic change in services. Drawing initially on Arnstein's ladder of citizen participation, the chapter seeks to develop a model of involvement and inclusion which promotes the idea of service users and carers being the agents of change within social work.

Chapter 6 addresses the implications of the analysis in previous chapters for social work and its emerging professional identity. Redefining social work within discourses of professionalism, the chapter traces the way social work interacts with other professionals, both within the UK and in relation to other professionals internationally. In particular it traces the development of interest with European models of social care such as pedagogy. It demonstrates the implications of pedagogy for new forms of practice.

Chapter 7 then provides a more detailed focus on social work in three European countries – Ireland, Denmark and the Czech Republic – and looks at the implications for practice in the UK. The conclusion seeks to draw together the key themes in the book and suggest a model for understanding the way social work in the UK is going which acknowledges the challenges of meeting the demands of service users, other professionals and the international social work agenda.

Learning features

The book seeks to engage the reader with the key issues raised by providing a number of key examples of the way particular approaches have been developed (for instance, see examples in Chapter 7). It provides a number of activities in each chapter to test the reader's understanding of the key issues and each chapter ends with a summary of the key issues, suggestions for further reading and a range of useful web addresses. For more detailed discussion of particular areas of social work practice readers are referred to other titles in the series such as:

Introduction to social work: Horner, N (2006) *What is social work?* Second edition.

The legal framework: Johns, R (2007) *Using the law in social work.* Third edition.

Service user involvement: Warren, J (2007) *Service user and carer participation in social work.*

Children and families: Jowett, M and O'Loughlin, S (2005) *Social work with children and families.* Second edition.

Chapter 1

A framework for understanding contemporary social work

This chapter will help you begin to meet the following National Occupational Standards for social work.

Key Role 1: Prepare for and work with individuals, families, carers, groups and communities to assess their needs and circumstances.

- Work with individuals, families, carers, groups and communities to enable them to analyse, identify, clarify and express their strengths, expectations and limitations.
- Work with individuals, families, carers, groups and communities to enable them to assess and make informed decisions about their needs, circumstances, risks, preferred options and resources.

Key Role 2: Plan, carry out, review and evaluate social work practice, with individuals, families, carers, groups, communities and other professionals.

- Develop and maintain relationships with individuals, families, carers, groups, communities and others.
- Help groups to achieve planned outcomes for their members and to evaluate the appropriateness of their work.

Key Role 3: Support individuals to represent their needs, views and circumstances.

- Advocate for, and with individuals, families, carers, groups and communities.
- Work with individuals, families, carers, groups and communities to select the best form of representation for decision-making forums.
- Enable individuals, families, carers, groups and communities to be involved in decision-making forums.

Key Role 4: Manage risk to individuals, families, carers, groups and communities.

- Balance the rights and responsibilities of individuals, families, carers, groups and communities with associated risk.

Key Role 5: Manage and be accountable, with supervision and support, for your own social work practice within your organisation.

- Carry out duties using accountable professional judgement and knowledge-based social work practice.
- Contribute to monitoring the quality of the services provided.
- Share records with individuals, families, carers, groups and communities.
- Deal constructively with disagreements and conflict within relationships.

Key Role 6: Demonstrate professional competence in social work practice.

- Work within the principles and values underpinning social work practice.
- Devise strategies to deal with ethical issues, dilemmas and conflicts.
- Contribute to policy review and development.

This chapter will also begin to help you achieve the National Occupational Standards in Community Development.

National Occupational Standards in Community Development

Key Role A: Develop working relationships with communities and organisations.

Key Role B: Encourage people to work with and learn from each other.

Key Role C: Work with people in communities to plan for change and take collective action.

Key Role D: Work with people in communities to develop and use frameworks for evaluation.

Key Role E: Develop community organisations.

Key Role F: Reflect and develop own practice role.

(PAULO, 2002 National Occupational Standards in Community Development Work. **www.fcdl.org.uk/ publications/documents/nos/standards**, retrieved 5 July 2006)

Introduction: The changing context of social work

Contemporary social work is facing a number of significant challenges as it seeks to establish a distinctive identity in the face of competing and emerging professions. For social work professionals, academics, people using services, and those training to become social workers, these challenges seem to multiply and become more complex with every new government initiative or crisis facing social work. This chapter seeks to conceptualise those changes and challenges within broader debates about social policy and legislation.

The search for a new identity for social work can be mapped against the recognition that social work has failed to meet the expectations placed on it by a combination of significant actors including the government, the media, people using services, other professionals and those involved with social work as a professional activity. Prior to 1997 many of these discourses were framed by a hostility to social work which was at least partly the outcome of the previous Conservative administration's hostility to public-sector organisations (Savage and Atkinson, 2001), public concern about the outcome of a number of inquiries into child deaths (Department of Health,1995), which social workers were held to be, at least partly, accountable for, and drives to create a professional identity which social work had previously been seen to be lacking (see Chapter 6).

One of the earliest initiatives under the Labour administration elected in 1997, to focus on renewing and making more accountable social work was *Modernising social services*, a White Paper presented to Parliament by the Secretary of State in the Department of Health in 1998 (Department of Health, 1998). Subtitled *Promoting independence, improving protection, raising standards*, the White Paper can be seen to encapsulate the government's key priorities for social work as it began its period of governance from 1997 to the present. The key problems identified by the White Paper included:

- protection – the improvement of safeguards to protect vulnerable children and adults;
- coordination – improving coordination between the different elements of the system;
- inflexibility – improving the ability of service to meet the needs of service users rather than service providers;
- clarity of role – a focus on expectations and standards;
- consistency – removing the imbalances between services provided across the country;

- inefficiency – a focus on minimising cost differentials between different providers.

While it is worth noting that many of these themes are at least the partial outcome of the move toward greater managerialism and control of public services, which can be traced back to the preoccupations of the previous administration (Dominelli and Hoogvelt, 1996), the themes did highlight a number of problems within existing provision which became the focus of policy initiatives over the next five to ten years. The White Paper drew particular attention to the need to promote independence, focus on individual need, achieve parity across the country in terms of provision, secure improvements to the looked-after care system – in particular a focus on improvements in safeguarding vulnerable children and adults, better training and greater public confidence in the work of social services. The latter would be achieved by improving the training of social workers and greater statutory regulation of social workers and social work agencies. At the heart of these proposals was the idea that these improvements should be attained through partnerships between the state, the market, the family and civil society or more specifically the third or voluntary sector (see Chapter 4) (Driver and Martell, 1999; (Johnson, 1999).

Policy and legislative framework

Those people looking for a comprehensive account of the legislative changes implemented since 1997 are referred to one of the numerous texts which provide an account of social work law (for example Brayne and Carr, 2005). They are also reminded that it was recently asserted that Labour had introduced over 3000 new criminal offences since its election in 1997 (Wilson, 2006). Clearly it would be impossible to do justice to such a wide-ranging legislative timetable within the confines of this book. They are in any event well dealt with in other titles in this series (Jowitt and O'Loughlin, 2005; Golightley, 2006; Horner, 2006; Williams, 2006; Johns, 2007). The discussion here is more concerned with the trends in social, political and legal policy which have impacted on social work. However, before these elements are drawn out it is important to draw attention to a number of the more significant legislative and policy developments which have occurred within the last ten years, or more specifically since the establishment of the modernisation agenda in 1998.

Arguably the Care Standards Act 2000 was the first and most significant of these developments. The Act was introduced because of concerns mentioned in the White Paper about the need to regulate social work and ensure a higher level of professional expertise among social work and social care staff. The Act established a new regulatory framework through the establishment of the General Social Care Council (GSCC) and the Commission for Social Care Inspection (CSCI). The GSCC replaced the Central Council for Education and Training in Social Work (CCETSW) and was charged with introducing a new qualification to replace the Diploma in Social Work (DipSW) and regulating the social work and social care workforce.

The year 2003 saw the introduction of the new degree in social work based on the National Occupational Standards for Social Work developed by the Training Organisation for Personal Social Services (later replaced by Skills for Care) and the

Benchmarking Statement for Social Work produced by the subject group for social work and social policy (Horner, 2006). The new social work degree has replaced the DipSW as the qualification for trainee social workers, although a small number of students are still registered to complete the DipSW. At the core of the new degree is a commitment to providing a generic training programme which will equip students to work across a wide range of social work settings. It focuses on six key roles (involving 21 units) which, it is argued, will enable the student to work effectively as a social worker and meet the requirements laid down in the modernising agenda. Each chapter in this book begins with an account of the key roles relevant to that chapter and suggestions as to how the reading and exercises can help the student achieve that level of competence required by the GSCC. However, because a key underpinning theme of the book relates to the role of other traditions in social work intervention such as community development and community action (Kendall, 2000), the chapters also refer the student to the National Occupational Standards set out for community work by the training organisation for community work (PAULO, 2002).

Understanding how policy development occurs

Hill (2005) has suggested that to understand the way policies are developed, enacted and implemented we need to be clear about the model of the policy process we adopt. He argues that we need to distinguish between policy content, policy output and the policy process itself. The first of these involves developing an understanding of the genesis and development of particular policies; policy outputs refers to the way particular services develop; and the policy process refers to the way decisions about particular policies are made and how they are shaped by those people and agencies responsible for implementing them. Such an approach enables us to understand how there may well be an imbalance between the perceived intentions of the policy-makers and the way policies are received and understood by the people for whom they are intended. In the current social work environment this means that it is not sufficient to simply assume that the intentions of the policy-makers are translated into practice but also that we may need to read beyond the rhetoric of the policy-makers to see if the policy really is geared to meet the needs of the groups for whom it is intended.

This is at the heart of this book. If the identified key themes of inclusion, inter-professionalism and internationalism are to be achieved we need to be able to evaluate the processes through which policy is formulated and implemented. For example, if policies are seeking to promote the involvement of people who use services, not just the professionals implementing policy, how is this realised? How can we make involvement real and not tokenistic? This dilemma is the focus of Chapter 5.

Hill (2005) also argues that to make sense of the way policy develops we need to understand the theories underpinning these approaches. He deals comprehensively with a wide range of theoretical approaches. For the purpose of this analysis it is sufficient to concentrate on three key theories: pluralism, elite theory and structuralism.

Hill describes pluralism (as defined by Dahl and his supporters) as a situation in which;

sources of power are unequally though widely distributed among individuals and groups in society. Although all groups and interests do not have the same degree of influence, even the least powerful are able to make their voices heard at some stage in the decision making process.

(Hill, 2005, p29)

Furthermore, any groups emerging through this process do so as representative of a wider societal view.

What does this mean for the analysis presented in this book? It suggests that although the groups of people with whom we as social workers interact are often the most marginalised and deprived within our society it should be possible to redress this unfairness or inequality through developing organisations which are representative of the people with whom we work. In this context both social workers as an interest or professional group and the people who use social work services (users and carers) should also be able to express their aspirations, and to an extent have them met, within the existing social system. It therefore provides us with an optimistic view of the potential for social change and there should be clear evidence that the policy intentions and the policy outcomes should be beneficial for those involved with social work.

Elite theory is described by Hill as representing an alternative to pluralism in so far as it suggests that power is concentrated in the hands of:

a variety of sources: the occupation of formal office, wealth, technical expertise, knowledge and so on. To a certain extent, these resources may be cumulative, but power is not solely dependent on any one resource.

(Hill, 2005, p37)

Elements of such associations include bureaucratic and business elites.

In analysing policies impacting on social work agencies, professionals and service users/carers this conception of policy development would suggest that we would need to see whether policy initiatives reflected the power interests of significant powerful groupings within the social work sector, in particular the professional groupings within social work and the regulatory and controlling bodies within social work such as professional associations, registration organisations (GSCC and CSCI) and administrative agencies such as Skills for Care and key government departments such as the Departments of Health and Education for Skills.

Structuralist explanations, including Marxism, emphasise the way power is mediated through economic agencies and the operation of systems of class stratification. In this conception actions, even of the most powerful groups, are determined by economic power so that structuralists *see political action as determined by powerful forces... which act as powerful constraints upon human action which have to be attacked to achieve fundamental change* (Hill, 2005, p42). Such an approach mirrors the analysis of radical social work and community work outlined in Chapter 2, and those seeking to tackle structurally determined policy drivers face the challenges outlined in Chapters 2 and 3.

What then are the key themes in recent policy developments around social work and how do they relate to these above analyses? The next section looks at three important areas of development within contemporary social work which throw a light on these discussions – policies around children and young people, people with learning disabilities and adults using social work and social care services.

Children and young people

It is not the purpose of this book to look in detail at the policy context in which work with children has developed. Readers wanting more information are referred to the companion volume by Jowitt and O'Loughlin (2005). The key policy framework for this area of work includes the Children Act 1989; the Children's Service Planning Order of 1996; *Quality protects* (1998); the *Framework for the assessment for children in need and their families* (DoH, 2000); the Children (Leaving Care) Act 2000; the Climbié Inquiry 2003; *Every child matters: Change for children 2004*; The Children Act 2004; and initiatives such as SureStart, Homestart and the recent Children's Centre initiative. For the purpose of this book, the focus will be on developments within services for looked-after children – particularly those around *Every child matters*. The key elements of *Every child matters* are:

- be safe;
- be healthy;
- enjoy and achieve;
- make a positive contribution;
- enjoy economic well-being.

Underpinning this approach is a commitment to partnership working (Chapter 6); the inclusion of young people using services (Chapter 5); and the development of a critical inter-professional practice (Chapters 4 and 6). In October 2005 the Commission for Social Care Inspection produced a report called *Making every child matter.* They suggested from their inspections of children's services that services needed to be made more accessible; that social workers needed to respond effectively to children in need and their families and that local authorities in particular needed to develop their role as corporate parents. In February 2007, the Commission for Social Care Inspection produced *Care matters*, which analysed children and young people's views of *Every child matters*. Among the key findings were that children wanted to be listened to more, have their different needs met, be kept safe and to have an effective social worker. Central to the last point was the idea of giving young people in care a say in decisions made about them.

At the same time as enhancing the rights of children and young people the government has also been strengthening the statutory framework for young people through the new structure provided in *Working together to safeguard children.* Following on from *Every child matters*, *Safeguarding children* emphasised the way in which:

> *A shared responsibility and the need for effective joint working between agencies and professionals that have different roles and expertise are required if children are to be protected from harm and their welfare promoted. In order to achieve this joint working, there must be constructive relationships*

between individual practitioners, promoted and supported by
- *the commitment of senior managers to safeguard and promote the welfare of children and*
- *clear lines of accountability.*

(HM Government, 2006, p10)

These themes of partnership, joint working and safeguarding vulnerable people find echoes in other legislation concerning learning disability and the needs of adults.

People with learning difficulties

The key policy agenda for people with learning difficulties is set out in *Valuing people: A new strategy for learning disability for the 21st century.* Published in 2001, the White Paper outlined the problems and challenges faced by people with learning disabilities, which, they argued, included: poor coordination and planning of services; insufficient support for carers; the lack of choice and control experienced by people with learning disabilities; unmet health care needs; inconsistency in service delivery and the frustrating lack of real partnership working across the health and social care sectors. It drew attention in particular to the problems faced by people from minority ethnic communities whose needs, 'are often overlooked' (p3).

The White Paper argued that central to improving the life chances for people with learning disabilities were four key principles: rights, independence, choice and inclusion. The key to achieving these objectives were the principles of advocacy and person-centred planning. Money was made available for the development of advocacy services and the White Paper said:

People with learning disabilities have little control over their lives, few receive direct payments, advocacy services are underdeveloped and people with learning disabilities are often not central to the planning process. The Government's objective is to enable people with learning disabilities to have as much choice and control as possible over their lives and the services and support they receive.

(Department of Health, 2001, p4)

People using adult services

The government produced a Green Paper (consultation paper) in 2005 which looked at the future direction of social care services for adults. *Independence, well-being and choice* sought to produce a new vision and framework for social care in which the government expressed its desire to:

Move toward a system where adults are able to take greater control of their lives. We want to encourage a debate about risk management and the right balance between protecting individuals and managing their own risks ... and to put people at the centre of assessing their own needs and how these can best be met.

(Department of Health, 2005a, p10).

The Green Paper suggested a range of outcomes for adult social care which included:

- *improved health – the promotion of good health and appropriate treatment and support;*
- *improved quality of life – access to leisure, social activities and lifelong learning and to universal, public and commercial services;*
- *making a positive contribution – active participation in the community;*
- *exercise of choice and control – maximising independence, choosing and controlling services, managing personal risk;*
- *freedom from discrimination and harassment – not being subject to abuse;*
- *economic well-being – access to sufficient income and resources;*
- *personal dignity – to be clean and comfortable, having available appropriate personal care.*

(Department of Health, 2005a, p26)

To achieve these goals the Green Paper suggested that it was important that people exercised control over the assessment of their own need through promoting direct payments and individual budgets over which the service user could exercise decision-making. In addition the Green Paper suggested the development of new models of service delivery and greater partnership between health and social care providers. A number of the respondents to the consultation on which the Green Paper was based indicated why these changes were necessary:

People don't have high expectations, just to be treated with a bit of dignity and respect with some of the opportunities the rest of us take for granted.

I've lost control of some things. I want control over my personal care.

The professionals really need to listen to people who use services.

(Department of Health, 2005a, p26)

In 2006 the government produced the White Paper *Our health, our care, our say* which provided a guide to the way in which consumers of health and social care services wanted to see services develop in the future. Patricia Hewitt, Secretary of State, in the introduction said that she noted:

how frustrating it is when the system seems to work against you rather than for you. Your answers give us great insight into the changes that need to be made, and in the government's white paper . . .Our health, our care, our say: a new direction for community services, we show how we are going to make them happen

(Department of Health, 2006, p3)

The White Paper was based on two major consultations in 2005 and from the responses from approximately 100,000 people. It promoted seven outcomes, which are:

- improved health and well-being;
- improved quality of life;
- making a positive contribution;

- choice and control;
- freedom from discrimination;
- economic well-being;
- personal dignity.

Other relevant initiatives

Since 1998 the government has been pursuing an agenda of tackling social exclusion and promoting social inclusion. This has been based on partnerships between statutory organisations, voluntary and independent organisations and the promotion of market mechanisms to generate prosperity and opportunity for all. The Department for Work and Pensions produced its seventh *Opportunity for all* report in October 2005. The report set out objectives to break inter-generational disadvantage and underachievement which included the eradication of child poverty in a generation, improving the quality of education to break cycles of deprivation, promoting work as the best form of welfare, supporting people to build personal assets and social capital (see discussion of social entrepreneurship in Chapter 6), providing security and independence in retirement and delivering high-quality public services.

The focus on the voluntary sector became increasingly important in recent policy developments (see Chapter 4). Early in 2007 the Charity Commission published its survey of the work of charities which provide public services. Their findings throw a light on the way in which the voluntary sector has come to play an important part in the delivery of public services. The report, *Stand and deliver*, notes how:

> almost one third of all public services delivered by charities are in the field of health and social care . . . Only 26% of charities that deliver public services agreed that they are free to make decisions without pressure to conform to the wishes of funders.
>
> (Charity Commission, 2007, pp3–4)

The report argued that in the current context charities needed to consider issues of independence and governance, funding and sustainability. These issues are discussed in detail in Chapter 4.

Sir Michael Lyons suggested in an article in the *Guardian* in October 2006 that, 'in areas such as social care it is difficult to see how the public services will achieve their goals . . . without a powerful alliance with the voluntary sector'. (http://society.guardian.co.uk/futureforpublicservices/story/, downloaded 13/11/06). Craig, Taylor and Parkes (2004) had previously noted that the government's emphasis on partnership was opening up opportunities for the voluntary sector. However, they suggested that government may be more interested in the service delivery role of voluntary organisations than more oppositional approaches. They point to the tensions in managing this relationship but expressed the view that the possibilities of a more mature rather than conflictual relationship existed. These issues are addressed in greater detail later in this book.

Table 1.1 illustrates the continuities in the above initiatives.

Table 1.1 Key themes: Continuities and developments

Theme	Originating policy/ legislation	Continues in	Future development
Regulation	Care Standards Act 2000	Independence, choice and well-being Safeguarding Children	
Training	Care Standards Act 2000	New social work qualification	Post-qualifying framework
Independence	Values in action	Independence, choice and well-being Our health, our care, our say	New adult services and Children's Workforce Directorate
Choice	Values in action	Every child matters Independence, choice and well-being	New Adult services and Children's Workforce Directorate
Well-being	Independence, choice and well-being	Every child matters Our health our care our say	New Adult services and Children's Workforce Directorate
Community	Values in action	Every child matters Opportunities for all	
Involvement	Values in action	Independence, choice and well-being Opportunities for all	New Adult services and Children's Workforce Directorate
Partnership	Values in action	Every child matters Our health, our care, our say	New Adult services and Children's Workforce Directorate

---

ACTIVITY 1.1

Table 1.1 shows how the plethora of policies which have emerged from the government since 1998 have important themes running through them, which provide an initial assessment that the intentions behind them are essentially benign. This seems especially so when taken together with the social exclusion agenda and the commitment to eradicate child poverty. Using Hill's typology of pluralism, elite theory and structuralism, indicate how these policy developments fit within his framework. Then after reading Chapters 2, 3 and 5, return to the table and assess your conclusions against these earlier conclusions.

Risk, risk avoidance and advocacy

This discussion highlights two key issues which are currently impacting on contemporary social work in the UK – issues of risk and advocacy or what Baistow has referred to as regulation and empowerment (Baistow,1994).

Independence, well-being and choice is important because it recognises that much of modern social care has become risk averse and reintroduces the idea that part of the task of social care workers should be to enable people using services to take risks. As Lupton has noted:

> *The language of risk is taking over from that of need or welfare in the literature on personal social services, such as probation, mental health and child care services, with risk assessment, risk management, the monitoring of risk and risk taking itself having become the raison d'être and organizing principle of agencies providing such services. Risk related discourses and strategies have taken on a key role in decision making about service delivery, including the rationing of services and decisions about need . . . individuals and groups are increasingly expected to engage in practices identified as ways of avoiding or minimizing the impact of risks to themselves.*
>
> (Lupton, 1999, pp98–9)

Yet counter-tendencies exist. Service users are increasingly demanding that they be allowed to make their own decisions, not have their choices mediated by the inter-vention of a professional. Consultations across the service-user spectrum are redolent with service users calling for the opportunity to take risks and be responsible for their own actions. In *Care matters* young people talk eloquently about their right to have more say in decisions made about them. One young person said, *Everyone wants to make decisions for me and it really hurts* (Commission for Social Care Inspection, 2007). Another said *children and young people need to be heard more*. In *Real voices, real choices* the services users consulted articulated strong views around the question of risk. The report says that *to reach their potential, an individual must be allowed – and supported – to take risks, have new experiences, and make mistakes* (Commission for Social Care Inspection, 2006, p12). They quote a participant in the *Shaping our lives* report who said that:

> *The right to manage risk should reflect the similar rights experienced by other people living in our community and society. Provided that access to help and advice is easily available I see no problem with this. Institutions with(in) the caring sector continually struggle with this in our blame culture and this is the main factor that has paralysed service providers to the point where they have become so ineffective radical change is required. Society punishes rather than learns from mistakes and this is very destructive. The balance for deciding on risk must swing drastically back to the individual service user.*
>
> (p13)

This commitment to choice and inclusion can be found in other areas. *Valuing people* talks of the need to avail even the most severely disabled person, with the right help and support, of the opportunity to *make important choices and express preferences about their day to day lives* (Department of Health, 2001, p24). *Independence, well-being and choice* recognises the dilemma posed by the need for protection but also argues for the establishment of *a debate about risk management and the right bal-ance between protecting individuals and enabling them to take their own risks* (Department of Health, 2005a, p28).

This discussion in turn highlights how it is important that people are able to articulate their own needs and concerns, and points to debates in the following chapters as to whether social work needs to revisit a more radical agenda.

Advocacy is an important means of achieving such aspirations for many people. Advocacy has been defined by the Independent Advocacy Campaign (seven key stakeholders representing people with physical, sensory, communication and profound multiple impairments) as *taking action to help people say what they want, secure their rights, represent their interests and obtain services they need* (Lewington and Clipson, 2004, p4).

Rapaport et al. (2005) have suggested that there are five core types of advocacy, which they describe as:

- legal advocacy – the broad range of methods and activities used by lawyers and other skilled individuals;
- class (collective, corporate or group) advocacy – when groups come together to speak up for and represent a larger group – for example, MIND, Mencap;
- self-advocacy – excluded people are empowered to speak for themselves – this is facilitated through providing opportunities to develop skills and gain knowledge and confidence to advocate on their own behalf;
- peer advocacy – people with similar experiences speak for each other;
- citizen (voluntary) advocacy – where a person with a need is linked to a volunteer to advocate on her/his behalf.

Underpinning this typology are the five key components:

- the assumption that each person has value;
- the acceptance of development theory – every person has the capacity for growth and learning;
- normalisation theory – encouraging people to achieve more valued social roles;
- consumer participation – increasing accountability;
- human and legal rights – people who use services are citizens with the same rights as others.

Atkinson (1999) has framed these key characteristics as being empowerment, autonomy, citizenship and inclusion, echoing some of the key themes outlined in the above discussion of the policy framework. Discussions of the potential of advocacy are often constructed by discourses on individual and social models of disability. Goodley argues that self advocacy sits uneasily with the individual model: if we *are told that impairment is all important and unsurpassable, then . . . self-determination can only go as far as these constructs of disability will allow: assumed inability hampering personal growth* (Goodley, 1997, p370). However, he suggests that the social model of disability permits a different approach:

> the social model encourages a context to be formed in which people can strive for self-expression, growth and determination . . . when an advisor sees people . . . not as passive individuals constrained by impairment, but as people actively striving for their own self-determination in the face of a society that

denies such rights, then self advocacy can be supported in a far more empowering manner.

(Goodley, 1997, p374)

This is a view supported by agencies working with users of services. People First workers say self-advocacy includes:

- speaking up for yourself;
- standing up for your rights;
- making choices;
- being independent;
- taking responsibility for oneself.

Aspis, quoting Dawson and Palmer (1997), argues that to self-advocate you need to resist practices which oppress you by challenging people in power, have the right to challenge others and be angry and challenge carers when the need arises (Aspis, 1997, p648). Elsewhere he (Aspis, 2002) argues that when self-advocacy groups successfully advocate for change it is often minor in nature; when more radical action is needed it can often cause problems. He quotes the example of Martin, who wished to move out of a group home to become more independent. The agency, which supported self-advocacy, was very hostile, which he attributes to them only seeing self-advocacy as valid within the boundaries set by their services (Aspis, 2002, p4). He argues that self-advocacy assumes *we are all working together and there is no conflict of interest* (p4). To Aspis, self-advocacy must include:

knowledge of how the institution and the system works; knowledge and use of the policy-making process in the institution and system; the understanding that service users and institutional or system staff and managers do not have equal power; knowledge and use of human and legal resources ... recognition of what level of change is needed, striving for changes that may include alternatives to the choices that are available ... one critical ingredient of understanding if self-advocacy has really worked is whether what has been asked for will be permanent or temporary.

(p6)

Aspis suggests the need for change in administration and institutional arrangements, local policy and statute if self advocacy is to achieve the impact it seeks.

ACTIVITY 1.2

1. *How does advocacy fit within the three policy frameworks discussed by Hill? Which is the most conducive to developing advocacy services?*
2. *Taking one of the policy areas discussed above – children and young people, learning disability and adults – explore three ways in which an advocacy strategy can be rationalised by the key legislation/policy discussed.*

Comment

You may want to draw on examples from your practice in answering these questions. Think back to the key roles and use them to explore how you would use advocacy in the circumstances you are working within.

Self-advocacy is only one of the approaches available within advocacy. Healy (2000) suggests that peer advocacy is:

a structured programme to assist young people... to develop the skills required to recognise, resist, report and replace bullying behaviours through representative advocacy.

It represents:

the establishment of a partnership which supports self-protective responses to abusive behaviour, not a dependent relationship where passivity is reinforced. The process of accessing and collaboration with a peer advocate are in themselves proactive responses on the part of the victimised individual, which will assist in the development of further effective behaviours.

Further, it challenges the dominance of social work in decision-making about children and young people. As an example he points to ASC (Advice, Advocacy and Representation Services for Children and Young People), which was established in 1992. The starting point was that advocates had the same status as other professionals. This approach is now growing across a range of settings including:

- specialist services responding to young people within certain social divisions;
- some wholly reliant on volunteers;
- others having paid workers.

Dalrymple argues that one of the advantages of advocacy is that it provides a potential focus on the notion of the 'committed practitioner' – *an ally with a personal commitment to social change* (Dalrymple, 2004, p186). She also suggests that child and youth advocates can be either professional or radical:

the professional advocate uses particular skills to motivate children and young people to ensure effective delivery of services. The radical advocate will challenge oppressive structures... the roots... though, are far from the radical traditions and, arguably for both professional and radical advocates their role is more compatible with the model of committed practitioner than other professional models.

(pp187–8)

This can be achieved by reducing the disempowering effect of the personal experiences of children and young people which has required them to need advocacy support. The advocate concentrates on the child or young person's feeling of self-worth and trying to enable them to strengthen the ability to control their lives. They in turn go further by seeking changes in the agency or wider systems which affect them. This is more like a systematic advocacy (Dalrymple, 2004, p192–3).

Boylan and Ing (2005) point out that providers need to promote greater awareness of advocacy services and young people's views need to be at the core.

They suggest that what young people want from their social worker is:

> *Someone you can trust and won't let you down… someone who will really stick up for you, who turns up when they say they are going to and is your friend* (female 14, residential care)
> An enduring relationship
> The appropriate exercise of power
> *She kicks arse, she's there for me* (Care Leavers Group)
> Independence from social services
> *She's not from social services so they take notice* (female aged 14, residential unit)

> (Boylan and Ing, 2005)

C H A P T E R   S U M M A R Y

This chapter has sought to chart some of the key issues facing contemporary social work. Following Hill (2005), it suggests a framework for analysing policies impacting on social work and looks at the way a number of consistent themes are beginning to emerge in the New Labour social policy discourse. These include issues of choice, control and independence. The chapter illustrates how these policy options are underpinned by contradictory discourses around risk, or rather risk avoidance and advocacy. The chapter provides a contemporary framework through which Chapters 2 and 3 will explore the way some of these dilemmas relate to the development of social work and the ways in which they can be resolved.

FURTHER READING

Hill, M (2005) *The public policy process.* 4th edition. Harlow: Pearson/Longman.
Provides a good account of the policy process, theories of power, organisational processes and inter-organisational processes.

Horner, N (2006) *What is social work?* 2nd edition. Exeter: Learning Matters.
A good introduction to the history and current practice of social work. Includes discussion of social work with all major groups of service users.

Jordan, B (2006) *Social policy for the 21st century.* Cambridge: Polity Press.
A thoughtful, if complex, discussion of the present and future direction of social policy in the UK. Includes a particularly good discussion of human well-being and social justice.

WEBSITES

Department of Health **www.dh.gov.uk/en/index.htm**

Social Exclusion Unit **www.cabinetoffice.gov.uk/social_exclusion_task_force/**
General Social Care Council **www.gscc.org.uk/home**

Chapter 2
Social work, community work and social change

This chapter will help you begin to meet the following National Occupational Standards for social work.

Key Role 1: Prepare for and work with individuals, families, carers, groups and communities to assess their needs and circumstances.
- Work with individuals, families, carers, groups and communities to enable them to analyse, identify, clarify and express their strengths, expectations and limitations.
- Work with individuals, families, carers, groups and communities to enable them to assess and make informed decisions about their needs, circumstances, risks, preferred options and resources.

Key Role 2: Plan, carry out, review and evaluate social work practice, with individuals, families, carers, groups, communities and other professionals.
- Develop and maintain relationships with individuals, families, carers, groups, communities and others.
- Help groups to achieve planned outcomes for their members and to evaluate the appropriateness of their work.

Key Role 3: Support individuals to represent their needs, views and circumstances.
- Advocate for, and with individuals, families, carers, groups and communities.
- Work with individuals, families, carers, groups and communities to select the best form of representation for decision-making forums.
- Enable individuals, families, carers, groups and communities to be involved in decision-making forums.

Key Role 4: Manage risk to individuals, families, carers, groups and communities.
- Balance the rights and responsibilities of individuals, families, carers, groups and communities with associated risk.

Key Role 6: Demonstrate professional competence in social work practice.
- Work within the principles and values underpinning social work practice.
- Devise strategies to deal with ethical issues, dilemmas and conflicts.
- Contribute to policy review and development.

This chapter will also begin to help you achieve the National Occupational Standards in Community Development.

National Occupational Standards in Community Development

Key Role A: *Develop working relationships with communities and organisations.*

Key Role B: *Encourage people to work with and learn from each other.*

Key Role C: *Work with people in communities to plan for change and take collective action.*

Key Role D: *Work with people in communities to develop and use frameworks for evaluation.*

Key Role E: *Develop community organisations.*

Key Role F: *Reflect and develop own practice role.*

(PAULO, 2002 National Occupational Standards in Community Development Work, **www.fcdl.org.uk/ publications/documents/nos/standards**, retrieved 5th July 2006)

Introduction: Reintegrating the radical into contemporary social work

As we saw in Chapter 1, social work is increasingly confronting pressures to refocus its gaze on the scope of individuals and to ignore or play down the way the problems individuals face are structured by broader social economic and political factors. In the UK the mixed economy of welfare (Johnson, 1999), increased marketisation of welfare services and the focus on assessment and regulation in social work practice (Humphries,1998) has led some to argue that any potential or radical practice has become marginalised. Yet at the same time there is an increase in recognition of the role of the user of welfare services (or more recently 'experts by experience') as an 'active agent'. Williams and colleagues have suggested we could see the emergence of a new welfare paradigm which:

> *emphasises the capacity of people to be creative, reflexive human agents of their lives, experiencing, acting upon and reconstituting the outcomes of welfare policies. It also points to the complex, multiple, subjective and objective social positionings that welfare subjects inhabit.*
>
> (Williams et al., 1999, p21; see also Chapter 5)

Below we will look at how social work activity is currently constructed within the parameters of the increasing poverty and social exclusion of social work's service users. Increasingly it has become recognised that social work can make a contribution to the process of social inclusion (Barry, 1998; Dominelli, 2004). Social work has a role in empowering people to overcome their exclusion through promoting forms of social inclusion. However, as Barry (1998) noted:

> *there seems to be a dichotomy between the philosophy behind the notion of social inclusion (which could be argued to be welfare-orientated and based on notions of a collective responsibility rather than individual blame, and the emerging trend within social work to move away from a more proactive welfare and collective approach to social problems and towards refocusing on reactive management of individual behaviour, irrespective of the wider social and economic context.*
>
> (Barry,1998, p9)

If anything, this trend has accelerated over the last eight years with New Labour's focus on the communitarian agenda of rights and responsibilities (Jordan and Jordan, 2001; Martell and Driver, 2002) and its increasingly punitive attitude to marginal groups and perceived anti-social behaviour.

At present, there is therefore a tendency to emphasise the control and management functions of social work without visibly examining or (re)examining the potential that social work may have for promoting processes of transformation. We need to address these problems by remembering again the issues raised by those theorists and activists who were promoting 'radical social work' or 'radical community work' in the early to mid-1970s and who have recently, at least, been seen to be swimming 'against the stream' of managerialism and the competency culture (Dominelli and Hoogvelt,1996; Pinkney, 1998; Clarke, Langan and Williams, 2001; Dominelli, 2004). These works provide the beginnings of a more systematic and structural framework against which we can evaluate social work's potential to engage with processes of change.

Remembering the radical alternatives: from casework to class struggle

An extensive selection of writings which could be said to fall within the umbrella of radical social work, including important literature on community work and community action, emerged around the mid- to late 1970s (examples include Leonard, 1975; Jones and Mayo, 1977; O'Malley,1977; Mayo,1980). To begin with we will examine those key collections which bore the sobriquet 'radical social work', specifically those by Bailey and Brake (1975), Brake and Bailey (1980) and Langan and Lee (1989), and to a lesser extent the work of the CaseCon collective which produced a magazine of the same name for a period in the mid- to late 1970s. We will then examine the literature which emerged from the Community Development Projects (CDPs) and radical community work around the same time.

Radical social work – what was (is) it?

Bailey and Brake (1975), in the introduction to the first radical social work collection, argued that their aim was to move social work beyond its then preoccupation with casework and its *over emphasis on pathological and clinical orientations to the detriment of structural and political implications* (Bailey and Brake, 1975, p1). This collection of readings promoted an advocacy/welfare rights approach, radical community action, and what Cohen called the 'politics of abolition', that is, maintaining a focus on abolishing the legitimacy of state organisations. In the same volume Leonard (1975) suggested that radical practice should be built around a process which involves working both within and against the structures in which the worker is employed. This he suggested involved a three-way process: the creation of dialogical relationships between worker and user; the development of group consciousness which entails 'the demystification of political structures and economic relations'; and the development of a complex range of organisation, administrative and planning skills (Leonard, 1975, p60 – the relevance of this analysis for contemporary practice will be discussed in later chapters).

This first collection drew extensively on the work of Paulo Freire (1972) and had a clearly oppositional stance to existing social work practice. However, although there is a focus on sexuality the paradigm addressed is essentially class based and there is no developed account of feminist or anti-racist struggles.

This absence was corrected in Brake and Bailey (1980). Wilson (1980) pointed to the tension between the personal and the political in any radical social work. As she argued:

> *it is not that help for the individual is inimical to social change (all political activists and movements have combined social aid for individuals for political campaigning); and social change cannot be brought about unless individuals feel that the politics will answer individual needs . . . but the problems that*

face social workers who are concerned with social change is the rather brutalised and ativised nature of the groups with whom they have the most part to deal; groups whose rebellion against their conditions of life often comes out not as rebellion but as personal disaster in the sphere of private life...Social workers never throw up an adequate strategy for dealing politically with these personal problems.

(Wilson, 1980, p39; see also Jordan, 1996 and discussion below)

Husband (1980) focused on the issues facing 'black' professionals and clients within social work, arguing that the cultural understanding of white UK social workers, when combined with the routinisation of their professional practice, *render white institutions particularly resistant to comprehending the new demands which they must meet in order to service multi-racial clientele* (p85).

This analysis was taken further in Langan and Lee (1989), who argued that one of the most important elements of the early radical social work texts was that they provided a critique of existing social work provision, and they pointed out that *one of the most useful things radicals can do is resist new attempts by the authorities to promote the idea that poverty is a problem of personal failure, rather than a social problem* (Langham and Lee, 1989, p15; see section on poverty and social exclusion below).

Hudson (1989) took forward the feminist critique of social work and pointed out how it had developed a critique of psychological paradigms in social work and argued for social work to develop a more meaningful account of the ways in which social inequalities impact on the personal and emotional lives of service users. She pointed out how statutory and professional power are issues with which feminists have sought to critically engage. She also pointed to the need for feminists to engage with men and points out how *the pursuit of great gender equality has sometimes been at the expense of recognising other oppressions, particularly those experienced by both black and working class women and by lesbians* (p93). Shar (1989) made a similar point when she argued that it is *not our responsibility to provide solutions for white women; they must find genuine ways of support by examining their own practice, ideas and motives* (p190). Hutchinson-Reis (1989) argued for the inclusion of a black perspective in social work education and training and the formation of a black workers' group.

Running throughout these texts is also a commitment to other forms of practice, particularly radical community action. Writing in 1975, Mayo had warned against the dangers of allowing the state to dictate the agenda, around community development (Mayo,1975, p135). In 1985 she argued for the continuing involvement of radicals in community work as a way of *criticising local services when they need to be criticised, yet defending the very existence of those services* (Mayo,1985, p275).

Similar arguments were also found in a number of other key texts during the 1980s. Jones (1983) sought to show how social work clients are separated off from those sections of the working class in employment. He pointed to the ways in which the focus of much social work is on the poor and disfranchised and argued that:

*for many clients, the sheer struggle to survive compels them to adopt the
most individualistic and introverted strategies which are completely at odds
with the traditions of collective action which have developed within the
organised working class both in their communities and in their work places.*

(Jones, 1983, p57; see comments of Jordan below
and discussion in Chapter 3)

Jones argued that socialists within social work should do their best to *maintain a
broad front of oppositional work* (p152). This would involve, he suggested, highlighting the inequalities which clients/service users face and arguing for the
democratisation of welfare services. He warned, however, against a simple process
of democratisation, pointing out that it can have negative consequences. Some of the
most marginalised groups of service users often face marginalisation within their
communities from within a *working class culture (with) long standing antagonistic
strands towards some clusters of the client population* (p155).

There are similarities here with some of the earlier arguments put forward by Bolger,
Corrigan *et al*. (1981). They argued for an approach which operates within and outside the state (see also Rowbotham, Segal and Wainwright, 1980) and pointed to the
way in which during the 1970s the welfare state had come to be perceived by the
general population as external to themselves, bureaucratic, paternalistic and depen-
dency-creating. This negative image, particularly among working-class people, created
a problem for socialists in that it *is absurd to expect that people who experience
humiliation on a day to day basis at the hands of the welfare* will then turn round and
defend it when the right wing *tries to dismantle it* (p151). Bolger *et al*. called for a
democratic restructuring of the welfare state suggesting a democratisation of the
client/worker relationship as well as the workers' relationship to the welfare state.
This democracy they suggested is *inextricably linked with the improvement of relationships, structure, politics, welfare policy and revolutionary change* (p154).
Arguably it was precisely this disenchantment with the welfare state that allowed
the Conservative government elected in 1979 to introduce neo-liberal policies aimed
at rolling back the state (Johnson,1999).

ACTIVITY 2.1

*Jane and Tom live in a three-bedroom flat in a high-rise block in Eastsea. They have
two children, Aaron who is 8 and Benji who is 5. The flat is damp and both children
have asthma. The family receive Income Support, but have no other source of income.
Their social worker has indicated that it is Jane and Tom's responsibility to ensure that
their children are healthy and that she will intervene if the family do not carry out
improvements to their property.*

Examine the above scenario and evaluate the following.

* *How a local authority social worker should intervene.*

* *Would a social worker with a more radical perspective adopt a different approach? If
so, how would it differ?*

Comment

Use the National Occupational Standards for Social Work and Community Work to look at the competencies both professions would expect a social worker to demonstrate within this work. The full sets of standards can be downloaded from the web addresses provided elsewhere.

An example of how these debates were played out across a state-sponsored community work project is provided by the Community Development Projects, which were funded by the Home Office in the early 1970s.

Community Development Projects 1970–74: from class struggle to difference and diversity

The Community Development Projects in Britain were announced following a statement from the Home Secretary in the Houses of Parliament in 1970 and were initially seen as *a neighbourhood based experiment aimed at finding new ways of meeting the needs of people living in areas of high social deprivation.* (Community Development Projects report,1974, p1). They were designed to intervene in areas of between 10 and 20 thousand people, but were concentrated in 12 areas ranging from Liverpool in the Northwest, Coventry in the Midlands, to Glyncorrwg in Glamorgan.

The first project was started in January 1970 and the last started in October 1972. The inter-project report written in 1974 noted that:

> *despite their wide diversity, projects have all identified similar symptoms of disadvantage indicating the now familiar profile of poverty. All areas do not share identical elements but most include:*
> * *lower than average incomes,*
> * *disproportionately high rates of unemployment,*
> * *high dependence on state benefits,*
> * *poor health records ... and poor housing.*
> (Community Development Projects,1974, p8)

The CDPs were a culmination of a decade of projects which had sought to deal with the rediscovery of poverty in the 1960s.

The projects were originally based on a social pathology model of urban deprivation in which it was assumed that:

> *problems of urban deprivation had their origins in the characteristics of local populations – in individual pathologies – and these could best be resolved by better field coordination of the social services, combined with the mobilisation of self help and mutual aid in the community even amongst those who experienced most difficulty in standing on their own two feet.*
> (Community Development Projects,1974, p1)

By the time the inter-project report was published in 1974 many of the projects had changed emphasis and had moved towards a structural analysis of the urban deprivation that the communities that they were dealing with suffered from. The report noted that:

> the problems of the 12 CDP areas are not reducible to problems of employment, housing, income and education. They are not isolated pockets suffering from an unfortunate combination of circumstances, they are a central part of the dynamics of the urban system and as such represent those who have lost out in the competition for jobs, housing and educational opportunity.
>
> (Community Development Projects, 1974, p52)

Such comments were borne out by the final reports from a number of the projects. The North Shields project's final report notes how the inter-project report for them *represented the decisive rejection of social pathology accounts of the problems of CDP areas and of the community therapy model, in the CDP's work, at least by the majority of CDPs.*

They note instead that North Tyneside *had adopted a class based account of these issues and origins* (North Tyneside CDP, 1974, Volume 3, 1974,p10). The arguments against social pathology were taken up and extended in the joint report, *Gilding the ghetto*, produced in 1977. The authors of *Gilding the ghetto* noted that the emphasis on tackling social needs in isolation inevitably distracts attention from the root causes of the problem by focusing attention upon personal deficiencies. (Community Development projects, 1977).

To counter these factors a number of projects developed an emphasis on community and group work solutions to the problems of their areas. The Benwell Project, in Newcastle, argued that it was valid to encourage people to engage in community action because their role was not to encourage people to, in their words, 'tolerate the intolerable'.

An example is provided by the work of the Benwell project, which argued that should people:

> make unreasonable demands, or even to demand the impossible, we would only answer that in the circumstances in which residents of Noble Street in Newcastle were placed themselves, they had no responsibility whatever to be reasonable if by that is meant learning to adapt to such circumstances. Indeed we would argue that the only reasonable reaction to such an environment is to do everything possible to escape from it. They did not create the slums; they did not want to live in them, the argument that there isn't enough money to do anything about it cannot and must not be taken seriously. For it is precisely this type of argument that led to the creation of the slums in the first place.
>
> (Benwell CDP, 1974, p45)

Similar discussions led some CDPs to adopt a more intransigently action-based approach. For example, North Shields argued for more projects to engage in the process of 'radical reformism'. They defined this as:

a class model of society, it is a process which involves fairly substantial change in one aspect of society but that in the end has not challenged the fundamental base of society. It tends to be most applicable in areas of social welfare, for example, the National Health Service implementation 1946 was a radical reformist measure, where it can alter the distribution of income in society and is an expression of the existence of organized class power, but it does not alter the fundamental structure of the social market economy model.
(North Tyneside CDP, 1974, p10)

This commitment to the radical reformist approach is described in detail in Volume 4 of the North Tyneside CDP's final report entitled *Organising for change in a working class area: The action groups.* The aims of this process are also through struggle to *make people conscious both of the process they are facing and their... power as a class to bring about unofficial changes* (North Tyneside CDP, 1974, p6 – see also Chapter 3).

In a review of the work of Coventry CDP, Bennington noted that *the progress of study for CDP and the locus of change need to be shifted therefore from deprived people or areas to the institutions or organisations of local and central government.* He went on to note that *to date the CDP appears to have only limited effectiveness as an instrument of social change* and that *it needs to locate its strategies within a longer time perspective and a historical view of change* (Bennington, 1974, p277).

Corkey and Craig (1978) note in their review of CDPs, that the analysis developed by the CDPs frequently brought them into dispute with their local authorities, and potential funders. As they note, *there is little support individual projects could call on outside the project areas in time of conflict.* They point to the ways in which working on individual issues threw out broader issues; for example, the 1976 housing campaign resulted in alliances between tenants and local authority unions.

On the basis of their analysis of the work developed by the CDPs with trade unions, Corkey and Craig concluded that *only the working class through its collective action, is in a position to defend its class interests against the operations of capital.* This leads them to generalise that:

traditional forms of community work are dangerous and that they tend to socialize working class areas into the existing economic system and community workers who are developing such strategies must be challenged about their attempt to control and dispel working class action and protest on behalf of the state.
(Corkey and Craig, 1978, p64)

Waddington located the experience of the CDPs as a watershed in the experience of community work in the 1970s. As he noted:

CDP fulfilled a prophetic function in plugging community work's theoretical and ideological cavities with a structural perspective at least for a time. But after the ending of CDP many community workers found it difficult to operationalise or apply the theory to their own practice, partly because the material produced by the CDPs has tended to be longer on analysis than on applications.

The experience of the CDPs should be seen as important because of the way in which they moved from an individual social pathology model of social deprivation to an analysis based on an understanding of class structure and of the interrelationship of industrial, economic and social policies. They were state sponsored and therefore to the extent that they supported the development of community action initiatives and developed a comprehensive critique of the operation of the state nationally and locally they can be seen as providing an important corrective to the individualising of social problems.

However, even within these criteria it seems clear that they were to some extent hindered by an overly deterministic class analysis of the role of the state. They sought to develop alliances between industrial and community groupings but seemed to have been guilty of putting forward an analysis which subsumed community interests below those of the industrial groupings with which they worked.

However, there is evidence from within the projects themselves that they made strenuous efforts to work with and empower the communities in which they were based. *Gilding the Ghetto* concentrates on how the state's commitment to tackling urban deprivation was merely empty rhetoric and argues that *the basic dilemma for the state remains the same, how best to respond to the needs of capitalism on the one hand and maintain the consent of the working class on the other* (p63).

And yet at the same time it is undeniable that the projects did extremely good and complex work with the communities in which they were based. The third and fourth reports of the North Shields CDP concentrated on the areas of group work within which they engaged. In Volume 4 of their report they demonstrate how the Percy Main Residents Group, a group made up of residents of a village near the River Tyne, maintained their militancy despite the fact that *the kind of tactics they used generated a lot of antagonism in the area because it affronted the notions of respectable and legitimate behavior of many of those who live there* (p39).

For example, a local GP wrote to the press complaining of the activities of the CDP and their small band of 'puppet followers'. He asked, *What is this country coming to when Local Authorities and Home Office combine to plant an extremist group like this in the community and allow to do as it pleases in the name of community development?* (cf. pp24–6, Vol. 4). Similar attitudes to what are perceived as oppositional groups continued throughout the 1980s and 1990s as witnessed by the public statement of Cllr Derek Allinson, then Chair of Cardiff City Council's Environmental Services Committee, who when discussing an application for funding from Adamsdown Law Centre (an independent free legal service controlled by the local community) said that to give the law centre money *would be like sending tanks to Saddam Hussein* (*South Wales Echo*, 2 November 1990).

The rationale for such an oppositional approach is provided in the Tyneside report, which notes that *collective work was regarded as desirable precisely because of a suspicion of case work approaches, suspicion not least of the long term effectiveness of any gains established in this way, even for individuals concerned* (p42).

They go on to argue how *individual case work legitimises the system and splitting is an essential mechanism for keeping things as they are* a factor which *was never squarely faced by North Tyneside CDP or anyone else for that matter* (p43). By 'splitting', they meant the individualisation of problems, so that people were prevented from seeing the structural causes of the problems they faced. Finally, the projects do not seem to have dealt explicitly with questions of gender or ethnicity. In fact, there seems to have been a tendency throughout the projects to subsume such issues within the umbrella of class oppression. Some commentators at the time questioned whether there was any substance to the idea that a radical community was ever effective. Vass suggests that this was a myth sustained by radical community workers themselves because of *a natural desire to believe in something regarded as new , different and alternative* (Vass, 1980, p3). However, despite the relatively short timescale within which the CDPs were operative it is undoubtedly true that they enabled a wide group of community activists to see the potential of generating change at the very least at local and regional level (South Wales Association of Tenants, 1982; Wales Social Security Campaign, 1990).

Themes in radical social and community work

The above discussion of radical social and community work suggests a number of key themes, which can, and should, be incorporated into discussions of current welfare practice. Briefly these are as follows.

- The need to reinsert class into our analysis. Phillips (1999) has noted the way that attention has shifted from the focus on class inequalities to the way gender, racial or cultural hierarchies undermine equal citizenship. Radical social work and its attendant literature can remind us of this need to connect all forms of oppression. The discussions of race/ethnicity and gender relations are important for social work, not just because they describe the social relations between groups/collectivities but because they also provide a means of grounding their practice.
- The need to democratise the organisations in which we work.
- The need to build a critical consciousness which can empower the individuals and collectivities with which we work.
- The need for a transformative vision which looks beyond the situations we currently face.

Focusing on poverty and social exclusion

One way in which social work has 'remembered' these concerns with class and structural factors has been an increasing recognition in the last ten years of the significance of poverty and social exclusion as determinants of the life chances of many of the service users with whom social workers engage. (Beresford and Croft, 1995; Beresford and Turner, 1997; Beresford *et al.*, 1999; Davis and Wainwright, 2005). The Law Centres Federation, a national body bringing together law centres (free legal advice centres) across the UK, argued in its 2000/1 annual report that their role was not simply to help individuals in need, they also had to combat deprivation and fight against the processes and structures – the barriers – that cause people to become excluded (p6). In a joint report with the Lords Chancellor's Office they listed among the key elements of their campaigning work:

- *Working with groups and local campaigns to target key problems affecting local people, for example where local services are threatened with closure.*
- *Linking individual problems with broader questions of local and national policy.*
- *Advising and assisting groups of clients where there is a common issue or problem.*
- *Helping local groups to develop the capacity to challenge the community's shared problems, for example supporting tenants' associations.*

    (Lord Chancellor's Department and Law Centres Federation, 2001, p42)

However, even this focus on social exclusion is itself problematic. Before embracing the concept we need to ask what we mean by social exclusion and how it can help us build strategies to improve the life chances of people using welfare services (Levitas,1998; Oppenheim, 1998; Byrne, 1999). Levitas (1998) has argued that the concept of social exclusion is problematic precisely because it dichotomises the experience of the included majority and the excluded minority and *draws attention away from the differences and inequalities among the included* (p7). Driver and Martell (1998) point out how New Labour's debates on social exclusion are framed by their commitment to communitarian notions of rights and responsibilities so that, *the government will fulfill its side of the bargain by helping the socially excluded find work; in turn the socially excluded must fulfill their own responsibilities by doing something about their condition* (p90; see also Byrne, 1998, and Chapter 4).

Levitas (1998) suggests that there are three distinct discourses around social exclusion, which she characterises as the redistributive discourse, the moral underclass discourse and the social integrationist discourse. Drawing on Levitas' analysis these discourses can be codified to suggest how they can 'fit' with a conceptualisation of social work. The results are presented in Table 2.1.

Table 2.1 Discourses around social exclusion – typical features and relationship to social and community work (adapted from Levitas, 1998)

Redistributive discourse	Moral underclass discourse	Social integrationist discourse
Poverty prime cause	Underclass culturally distinct	Narrow definition exclusion – emphasises paid work
Increase in benefit levels	Focus on behaviour of poor	Does not imply increase in benefits
Can valorise unpaid work	Implies benefits are bad	Obscures inequalities between paid workers
Posits citizenship as obverse exclusion	Ignores societal inequalities	Obscures gender inequalities

Broad critique of inequality, not just limited to material inequality	Gendered discourse about idle, criminal young men and single mothers	Obscures class inequality
Focus on processes which cause inequality	Unpaid work unacknowledged	Unable to deal with question of unpaid work
Implies radical reduction of inequality and redistribution of societies' resources	Dependency on state problematised, personal economic dependency not problematised	Ignores unpaid work and its gendered distribution, implies increase in women's workload, undermines the legitimacy of non-participation in paid work
Community action, self-organisation	**Casework, statutory, dependency creating**	**Community development, interventionist, top-down**

Each of these discourses has different implications for social and community work. The theory of social exclusion which underpins our interventions determines our ability to engage with service users in ways which lead to their empowerment rather than their oppression. For example, a moral underclass analysis would lead us to view service users in terms of their deficiencies and social pathology and would be likely to result in us problematising service users rather than looking at the broader social factors which impact on them. A social integrationist discourse is likely to lead us to see reintegration into the labour market and policies which aim to achieve this goal (Working Families Tax Credit, Disability Tax Credit, personal advisers, job training) as being the most fruitful outcome. A redistributionist discourse is the one which is more likely to focus our attention on wider structural factors, minimise any tendency toward pathologising the service users we work with and focus our attention on social change and societal redistribution.

Jordan (1996) argues that the choices open to people in poverty are in any event more constrained than those from more affluent communities and that *these processes of social exclusion through community formation and 'voting with the feet'* (p169) indicate that the life chances of the affluent and the dispossessed are constrained by their occupation of 'communities of choice' or 'communities of fate'. He suggests that the latter should not be characterised as *passive, anomic or resigned* but should be seen as generating *strong resistance cultures* which involve both *solidaristic and supportive association and opportunistic, predatory action against the residents of 'communities of choice'* (p174). He points to the way in which these processes impact disproportionately on women and people from minority ethnic communities. He argues that:

> Poor women, and especially women from ethnic minorities, constitute the basis for 'community' and hence for social policies that try to define the relationship between public providers of welfare services and their clienteles in terms of 'partnership'.
>
> (p185)

This is an interesting attempt to introduce the notion of welfare recipients as active agents who consistently negotiate space for change. It connects with some of the concerns expressed within radical social and community work about the capacity of people to create collective solutions to the problems they face. Indeed, Jordan points to the way in which these women often have to resist dual pressures in that public authorities exploit the *community of women in the very manner that individual men exploit their partner* (pp182–3). This fits with the attempts also current to develop a new 'cultural perspective' on welfare, which shifts *attention from the spheres of the market, and of the administrative state, to the networks and social relations of society itself* (Freeman et al., 1999, p280). It is also consistent with Williams, Popay and Oakley's (1999) suggestion that we need to develop a new paradigm of welfare.

Lister sees poverty as spelling *exclusion from the full rights of citizenship in the social political and civil spheres and undermines people's ability to fulfil the public and private obligations of citizenship* (Lister, 1998, p29). She argues that there is a need to distinguish between a person's capacity to be a citizen and to act as a citizen, and that to tackle poverty and exclusion and promote inclusion we need to promote the idea of active citizenship (Lister,1997, 1998). We will return to these arguments later.

ACTIVITY 2.2

Look again at the situation Jane and Tom find themselves in (Activity 2.1). Using Levitas' typology of social exclusion, indicate:

- *how the models of social exclusion can be used to understand the circumstances they find themselves in;*
- *which model of social exclusion a radical social or community worker would use to underpin their intervention with the family.*

Comment

Levitas categorises social exclusion as being of one of three types; redistributive, social integrationist or moral underclass. Apply these typologies and think about their implications for social or community work practice.

From radical social work to critical social work

Can we therefore use these insights to construct a transformatory and critical social work? Langan (1998) has suggested that the radicalism that was seen in social work practice in the 1970s became transformed in the 1980s to a top-down process in which a progressive agenda, to the extent it existed, was promoted from above – by academics and managers. While the 1990s saw the promotion of anti-discriminatory/ anti-oppressive practice, from both practitioners and the regulatory body, CCETSW, she argued that *the radical commitment to liberation appeared to have been transformed into a mechanism for regulation* (Langan,1998, p215). Mullaly (1993) argues for a structural social work which *views social problems as arising from a specific societal context – liberal/neo-conservative capitalism – rather than from the failings of individuals* (p124).

Healy (2000) argues that the prevalence of such an approach is not accidental but that critical social work has become marginalised because it has failed to re-evaluate its own practice. In particular, she suggests that critical or radical social work privileges 'certain practice contexts' over others in a way which fails to take account of the way in which social workers minimise the implications of power relations in their practice; they oversimplify the power differential between workers and users and they devalue some forms of change activity. She says:

> *Radical analyses can overlook the emancipatory potential in everyday social work practices by establishing standards that devalue much of the change activity in which social workers are involved. At the same time, the emancipatory potential of other practice contexts is exaggerated because of a failure to acknowledge the extent to which the historical context of social services impacts on the kinds of practices that are possible.*
>
> (Healy, 2000, p5)

This is an important corrective to an overly naïve approach to the issue of social change and social transformation and in some ways replicates earlier invocations to work 'in and against the state' and Mullaly's argument that we should work *within (and against) the system* by using social work skills and techniques in such a way that we *demystify it by discussing its origins, purpose . . . and by encouraging service users to ask questions* (Mullaly,1993, p174).

Dominelli and Hoogvelt (1996) have argued that an emphasis on competence in social work has been part of the process of 'bureaucratisation of quality' which has afflicted social work and which in part is a response to changes in the mixed economy of welfare over the period since 1979. They suggest that:

> *the breaking up of complex social work tasks which require fine professional judgements be made, reflects an attempt to move the work away from autonomous critical reflective practitioners, for the critical reflective practitioner is a worker who is capable of independent judgement and who wields a certain degree of power as a professional over the employer and any given client in defining the task to be done in any particular situation.*
>
> (p56)

Social work is therefore currently the site of a battle of ideas: on the one hand, those who are seeking to reduce social work as an activity to a set of professional competencies, and on the other, to a group of people who are seeking to create a form of social work which is based on notions of reflective and critical practice (Gould, 1989, Yelloly, 1995; Dominelli and Hoogvelt, 1996).

A key to this debate within social work is the debate around anti-discriminatory/anti-oppressive practice (Thompson, 1997). Cornwell identified the reasons why anti-discriminatory practice/anti-oppressive practice became so important in contemporary British social work when she argued:

> *that since the mid 1980's there has been a growing determination in the field of social work education to shift the emphasis from racism out there to racism in here. This determination is in response to the recognition that racism is not*

so much a nasty habit that other people indulge in, as a particularly unpleasant malpractice in which we are all actively, collectively and often unconsciously engaged, through the racism inherent in structural and institutional aspects of our society. The issue is one of social justice.

(Cornwell, 1993, p92)

Thus, social work should have a focus not just on acknowledging or understanding racism/discrimination, but on challenging and seeking ways of overcoming such racism/discrimination.

Dominelli (1999) has suggested that social workers have responded to the increased privatisation of social work, an accompanying loss of professional autonomy and a dissipation of their professional role in three ways: through accommodation, escapism or resistance. Accommodation is characterised by the social workers' engagement with the new contracting culture in a naïve belief that *they will continue to provide a service that is more consistent with a public service ethos and social work's professional ethics* (p20). Escapism strategies are pursued by those who feel professionally disempowered and respond by looking for work outside the public sector. Rather than naïvety, their position is characterised by a cynicism derived from their view of *the system's capacity to respond appropriately to any challenge which is mounted against it* (p20). The resisters are also characterised by their feelings of alienation and disaffection from the system. The difference is in their response. They take an activist role in challenging the decisions of the agencies within the system. Dominelli says:

The activities of women, black people, gay men, lesbian women and disabled people in raising the failure of social services to respond appropriately to their needs are examples of resisters who have sought to change the situation that service users face.

(Dominelli, 1999, p21)

This schema provides an interesting means of distinguishing the responses of social professionals to the challenges faced by globalisation, privatisation and the dampening down of the radical agenda which was so much at the forefront 20 years ago. However, it oversimplifies a complex reality. Social workers are still, if to a much lesser degree, working within the system (Rowbotham, Segal and Wainwright, 1980; Mullally, 1993). In addition, Dominelli's account is guilty of over-concentrating on the public sector. Many of the changes she describes have been experienced by state social workers. However, a consequence of privatisation has been the expansion of social work into other areas of the mixed economy. NGOs or voluntary-sector organisations have to some extent benefited from the disillusion of state workers. Forms of radical and alternative practice are, if not flourishing, at least with strong enough roots to ensure that emancipatory forms of practice can still be found. I would suggest that Dominelli's typology could be expanded to encompass a more diverse range of practices. The typology could therefore be reconstructed as in Table 2.2.

Table 2.2 Models of practice

Type of practice response	State social work (child care)	Anti-racist work	Social/community action
Accommodation	Child protection/court work	Race equality councils	Councils of community service
Escapism	Voluntary sector	Multi-cultural festivals	Non-state service providers
Resistance	Organisations of young people in care	Anti-racist organisations	Social action projects

Dominelli (1998) suggests elsewhere that anti-oppressive practice can provide a way of helping people organise their responses to the questions of equality and social justice posited by the theorists of 'radical', 'structural' or 'critical' social work. It is, she suggests:

> *Intimately bound up with notions of improving the quality of life or well-being of individuals, groups and communities. This concern lends it a holistic mantle, which encompasses all aspects of social life – culture, institutions, legal framework, political system, socio-economic infrastructure and interpersonal relationships which both create and are created by social reality ... [this has led people to] look for bonds of solidarity which acknowledge the different starting points held by groups of people working towards a common aim.*
>
> (Dominelli, 1998, pp5–6)

An example of the way in which social work has sought to address these issues of marginalisation can be seen in the work of the ECSPRESS network – an initiative supported by the European Union which brought together social workers and other social professionals from across Europe who were concerned about the threat of social exclusion (Lorenz, 1997; Barry and Hallett, 1998; Marynowicz-Hetka, Wagner, and Piekarski, 1999). The ECSPRESS network symbolised a growing commitment to the development of networks of social professionals and the establishment of training and education initiatives which sought to improve inter-country cooperation. Walter Lorenz, writing in 1997 about the future facing the ECSPRESS network, argued that there were a number of challenges confronting us if we wanted to develop a European perspective in social work, particularly as:

> *a broader European perspective relativises the traditional national understanding of the duties and responsibilities of a particular professional group.*
>
> (Lorenz, 1997, p28)

The challenge this poses was also the subject of a CCETSW/ National Institute of Social work seminar held in 1995 (Connelly and Stubbs, 1997). A recent report to CCETSW (the social work accrediting body in the UK) drew attention to the *ways* in which, *wider European and international developments will ... have a bearing on UK policy and practice* (p10). This need to Europeanise and internationalise our approach to social work is dealt with more extensively in Chapter 7.

Conclusion: Promoting inclusion

Where does this leave us? The above analysis suggests that we can learn from the theorists of radical social and community work and apply the lessons learned to the complex problems of poverty and social exclusion, which structure the experience of so many users of welfare services. Our focus should be on inclusion, on how we bring people into society in a way which acknowledges, and tackles, the severe marginalisation and disadvantage they suffer and which recognises that these processes of exclusion are structural to the societies in which we live. Clearly we need to develop a multi-dimensional response to the multi-dimensional problems outlined above. But this is more than just producing joined-up solutions. Joined-up solutions are often more discriminatory than fragmented responses as they enhance the power of the politicians and professionals and further marginalise the excluded.

Any solutions we develop will need to be based on a number of principles, which can be summarised as the 'A–F of inclusion'. These are:

- **Active citizenship** by and large people are not passive, they merely lack the belief in their own capacity and the knowledge and skills to achieve change.

- **Bringing people in** overcoming the 'them and us' mentality which so often creates impasses in attempts to revitalise areas; normally people express anger and frustration because they are not being heard, not because they are.

- **Capacity building** to overcome this passivity people need to be given the resources – physical, material and economic – to change their situation.

- **Doing things for themselves** this means local authorities, key agencies and voluntary organisations not imposing their agendas but allowing people the opportunity to make their own mistakes and learn from their experiences.

- **Empowering people and promoting equality** this is more than giving people information or £100 to support their community newsletter. This means really listening to people, hearing what they say and taking action together to bring about change. We cannot empower people – they can only do that themselves. Equality should be our central concern because that is the only way in which we will overcome the discrimination and oppression which underpins people's experience of exclusion.

- **Fear, or rather, overcoming fear** partnership and real involvement are challenging but they do work; we all need to lose our fear of the excluded.

Making these principles real can provide a way for us to link together the political and social analysis in 'radical social work' with current concerns about marginalisation and exclusion and provide an agenda for the future direction of social work or the social professions.

C H A P T E R   S U M M A R Y

This chapter began by looking at the way the control and management function of social work has become preponderant in current social work discourses and how consequently the more liberatory and empowering elements of social work have become marginalised. In an attempt to redress this imbalance the chapter looked at the histories of radical social and community work and demonstrated the continuities between them. It suggested that debates around poverty and social exclusion provided a way of refocusing the attention of both professions to the wider structural issues with which users of social work services contend. Using Levitas' typology of social exclusion the chapter looked at how social and community work would need to refocus their orientations to a more egalitarian, redistributive approach and thus reclaim the agenda around social justice. Chapter 3 builds on these insights and explores the continuities and differences between social and community work.

FURTHER READING

Healey, K (2005) *Social work theories in context*. Basingstoke: Palgrave Macmillan.
A complex but interesting account of the way in which social work theory informs practice. It has a useful chapter on radical and anti-oppressive practice and another chapter on creating frameworks for practice.

Levitas, R (1998) *The inclusive society*. Basingstoke: Macmillan.
A good, clear analysis of how discussions around social exclusion are not neutral but have important implications for how we as social or community workers relate to people experiencing exclusion.

Chapter 3
Squaring the circle – from the individual to the collective?

This chapter will help you begin to meet the following National Occupational Standards for social work.

Key Role 1: Prepare for and work with individuals, families, carers, groups and communities to assess their needs and circumstances.
- Work with individuals, families, carers, groups and communities to enable them to analyse, identify, clarify and express their strengths, expectations and limitations.
- Work with individuals, families, carers, groups and communities to enable them to assess and make informed decisions about their needs, circumstances, risks, preferred options and resources.

Key Role 2: Plan, carry out, review and evaluate social work practice, with individuals, families, carers, groups, communities and other professionals.
- Develop and maintain relationships with individuals, families, carers, groups, communities and others.
- Help groups to achieve planned outcomes for their members and to evaluate the appropriateness of their work.

Key Role 3: Support individuals to represent their needs, views and circumstances.
- Advocate for, and with individuals, families, carers, groups and communities.
- Work with individuals, families, carers, groups and communities to select the best form of representation for decision-making forums.
- Enable individuals, families, carers, groups and communities to be involved in decision-making forums.

Key Role 4: Manage risk to individuals, families, carers, groups and communities.
- Balance the rights and responsibilities of individuals, families, carers, groups and communities with associated risk.

Key Role 5: Manage and be accountable, with supervision and support for your own social work practice within your organisation.
- Carry out duties using accountable professional judgement and knowledge-based social work practice.
- Contribute to monitoring the quality of the services provided.
- Share records with individuals, families, carers, groups and communities.
- Deal constructively with disagreements and conflict within relationships.

Key Role 6: Demonstrate professional competence in social work practice.
- Work within the principles and values underpinning social work practice.
- Devise strategies to deal with ethical issues, dilemmas and conflicts.
- Contribute to policy review and development.

It also meets the requirements of the *Benchmarking Statement for Social Policy and Social Work* in that it reflects the key issues raised by the following:

2.4 Although social work values have been expressed at different times in a variety of ways, at their core they involve showing respect for persons, honouring the diverse and distinctive organisations and communities that make up contemporary society and combating processes that lead to discrimination, marginalisation and social exclusion. This means that honours undergraduates must learn to:

- recognise and work with the powerful links between intra-personal and inter-personal factors and the wider social, legal, economic, political and cultural context of people's lives;
- understand the impact of injustice, social inequalities and oppressive social relations;
- challenge constructively individual, institutional and structural discrimination;

- help people to gain, regain or maintain control of their own affairs, insofar as this is compatible with their own or others' safety, well-being and rights.

This chapter will also begin to help you achieve the National Occupational Standards in Community Development.

National Occupational Standards in Community Development

Key Role A: Develop working relationships with communities and organisations.

Key Role B: Encourage people to work with and learn from each other.

Key Role C: Work with people in communities to plan for change and take collective action.

Key Role D: Work with people in communities to develop and use frameworks for evaluation.

Key Role E: Develop community organisations.

Key Role F: Reflect and develop own practice role.

(PAULO, 2002 National Occupational Standards in Community Development Work. **www.fcdl.org.uk/ publications/documents/nos/standards**, retrieved 5th July 2006)

Introduction

In Chapter 2 we looked at how social and community work shared some common theoretical and policy histories which would allow us to develop in this chapter a clearer overview of the way in which the similarities of both approaches could be systematised. This will allow us to begin to outline a potentially new form of welfare practice which can equip us to operate in the constantly changing welfare environment we are currently experiencing. This chapter will seek to explore these similarities, and differences, and begin to produce a framework for this new practice which will be fully articulated in the Conclusion.

Such an approach must begin by seeking to show how the concern with the individual, which is often held to characterise social work, maps against the concern for the communal or collective, which is often attributed to community work; or to rephrase the dilemma: casework or community work?

A number of writers have suggested that to understand the history of social work we need to see how it developed as an approach to the alleviation of social problems at the end of the nineteenth and beginning of the twentieth centuries and how approaches to social work were defined through the work of agencies such as the Charity Organisation Society and the Settlement Movement. The former was characterised by an approach to social work which focused on the relief of individual distress, which became known as 'casework', and the latter by approaches which stressed the more structural causes of social problems – the community development approach (Pinkney, 1998; Kendall, 2000). Such a distinction always seemed slightly nebulous in that for the user of social services 'problems' were always framed by both factors. Often a 'problem' impacted on the user and their family directly, personally and immediately and the social worker was required to intervene to resolve the 'problem' as it was defined at that particular time. However, many such 'problems' were not resolvable immediately and required a more systematic intervention which often meant the social worker dealing with other agencies, acquiring additional resources, linking with other social institutions. The 'problem' required in other words a structural or at least communal approach if it was to be resolved.

As we saw in the last chapter, writers on social work have understood this dilemma for some time even if it was more commonly associated with the 'radical' traditions within social work. More recently writers from the UK (Oliver, 1996; Hanmer and Statham, 2001; Thompson, 2001; Dominelli 2004), Canada (Mullaly, 1997; Gil, 1998) and Australia (Ife, 1997; Healy, 2000; Fook, 2002) have all sought to demonstrate how the individual experience is mediated through a broad range of social, political and structural factors. They have demonstrated how an individual's circumstances only change, in any lasting and meaningful way, if change also occurs in their wider environment – their housing, living circumstances – but more particularly in their own understanding of how their experience is shaped by wider social forces (Freire,1972).

Community work has often focused largely on these wider factors, supporting people to take action to change their circumstances and equipping them with the knowledge and skills to make these changes sustainable over time. Community workers have not always been so good at understanding the private, individual side of these campaigns, particularly that community work which has been driven by a broader political agenda and underpinned by a Marxist analysis of change (see Chapter 2). However, it is again important not to oversimplify this analysis and feminist and anti-racist community workers have often sought to integrate the personal experience into the wider social change perspective (Mayo, 1972; Dominelli, 1990; Ledwith, 1996).

These debates are reflected in the two sets of occupational standards produced by the Training Organisation for Personal Social Services (TOPSS; now Skills for Care) and PAULO, the training organisation for community development (see Table 3.1).

Table 3.1 Comparison of National Occupational Standards across social and community work

Social work		Community development	
Key Role 1	Prepare for and work with individuals, families, carers, groups and communities to assess their needs and circumstances	**Key Role A**	Develop working relationships with communities and organisations
Key Role 2	Plan, carry out, review and evaluate social work practice, with individuals, families, carers, groups, communities and other professionals	**Key Role B**	Encourage people to work with and learn from each other
Key Role 3	Support individuals to represent their needs, views and circumstances	**Key Role C**	Work with people in communities to plan for change and take collective action
Key Role 4	Manage risk to individuals, families, carers, groups and communities	**Key Role D**	Work with people in communities to develop and use frameworks for evaluation
Key Role 5	Manage and be accountable, with supervision and support for your own social work practice within your organisation	**Key Role E**	Develop community organisations
Key Role 6	Demonstrate professional competence in social work practice	**Key Role F**	Reflect and develop own practice role

Key Role 1 of the TOPSS NOS refers to working with individuals and communities while the PAULO standards refer to working with communities and organisations. Key Role 2 talks about evaluating and reviewing practice while Key Role B refers to helping people learn from each other. The interface between the two activities can be clearly seen in Key Roles 3 and C. The former speaks of the need to help people advocate and of the importance of social workers helping people represent their *views and circumstances*, while the latter talks about community development helping people take collective action and plan for change. The difference here is on the extent of the change process, not on its desirability (see Chapter 4 for a fuller discussion of the relationship between advocacy and empowerment).

Key Roles 4 and D focus on another key element in practice: the relationship of risk to professional activity. The social work literature often sees risk as problematic and in need of management. The community work literature instead sees evaluation as the key to improving effectiveness and enhancing collective power. The difference in this case can be theorised as being between risk management and risk promotion. Key Roles 5 and E may appear to have something in common in that they both focus on accountability. However, this again can be seen as coming from different perspectives, with social work's ideas of accountability focusing on accountability to the agency as employer, and community work's focus on accountability of and to the agencies with whom community workers work. Here the agency is seen as a means of articulating the change process and creating alternative forms of organisation which enhance the possibility of empowering the people with whom the community worker works. Again this may be down to different perceptions of the meaning of participation and we will return to this debate in Chapter 5. Key Roles 6 and F show a similar commitment to reflective and by definition accountable practice with both focusing on issues of diversity and discrimination.

The points of contact between the two professional activities may now be becoming clearer. However, before we attempt to conceptualise these distinctions it will be useful to look at what current discourses within social and community work tell us about the professions.

ACTIVITY 3.1

Jane and Ed live in a two-bedroom flat in the poorest area of Northerndown. Their landlord requires them to leave their flat because he says he needs it for another tenant. Jane approaches you for assistance. They have family close by and want to stay in the property. Your manager agrees that you should offer them support. Identify which of the key roles you would utilise in your work to support the family, differentiating between the social work and community work roles.

Comment

Return to the key roles. Use Table 3.1 to help you compare the different roles within social and community work.

The meaning of community

'Community' is one of the most widely used and often ill-defined terms in social science. In a similar way to which 'empowerment' is often used inappropriately, 'community' is often used indiscriminately to enhance the appeal of policies, which may themselves be unattractive – community policing, community safety, community partnership, community school (particularly when the old Borstals were renamed in this way). Day notes that:

> community signifies something vague and ill-defined, an excuse for not thinking hard enough about what exactly it is that people have in common...'community' is a highly problematic term, alluring in its promise but to be approached with extreme care.
>
> (Day, 2006, p2)

What then does it mean? Bauman (2001) sees community as a counterbalance to the atomisation and individualisation of a globalising world and as way through which we can gain or regain control. He concludes his discussion of community by reflecting that:

> We all need to gain control over the conditions under which we struggle with the challenges of life – but for most of us such control can be gained only collectively.
>
> (Bauman, 2001, p149)

This debate around the purpose of community is not new. Ferdinand Tonnies used the idea of community to describe the transformation in social relationships brought on by modernisation. He described two processes, *Gemeinschaft* and *Gesellschaft*. The former he suggested is characterised by *emotional commitment, loyalty, emphasizing common ties and feelings and a sense of moral interdependence and mutual obligation*, the latter by *artificial, impersonal, economic relationships designed and controlled by others* (cited in Brueggemann, 2006, p126). *Gemeinschaft* is held to characterise pre-industrial social relations and *Gesellschaft* industrial social relations. However, much of today's discourse around community, particularly communitarianism harks back to these idealisations of community, especially *Gemeinschaft*.

Burns, Hambleton and Hoggett (1994) suggest that it is necessary to distinguish between different conceptions of community. They posit five meanings of community:

- *community as heritage;*
- *community as social relationships;*
- *community as the basis for collective consumption;*
- *community as the basis for the most effective production and provision of local public goods;*
- *community as the source of influence and power.*

They go on to suggest that within these conceptions it is also useful to see a further distinction between communities of interest and imagined communities or communities of place. They suggest these can be defined as:

- **Communities of interest** *reflect the common material concerns or characteristics of members and/or the common issues around which they group.*
- **Imagined communities** *communities formed on the basis of common interest but of common identities. The basis of social bonds is likeness or similarity.*
- **Communities of place** *particular types of imagined community territorially based and can be mobilised to defend local interests.*

They stress, however, that people may have multiple identities and linkages.

Jordan (1996) makes a further distinction between 'communities of fate' and 'communities of choice'. The first reflect the restrictions disadvantaged communities face and the social polarisation that is often characteristic of them; the latter the greater freedom accorded those successful in an increasingly polarised society.

These different conceptions of community provide us with an important reminder of the complex reality with which we are dealing and, in particular, suggest that when we reflect on the models of community work outlined below we should be aware that the types of intervention or strategy we choose need to take account of these different meanings. For example, our method of intervention may differ if we are seeing community as a site of struggle over the allocation of power or as an imagined community without a physical presence. Equally if we are to equip people to work for change we will want to challenge the idea that they are located in a community of fate. We need to help people believe in their potential to change their situation by encouraging them to see themselves as capable of generating alternative futures.

ACTIVITY 3.2

Which of the conceptions of community outlined above best describe the community in which Jane and Ed live (see Activity 3.1)?

What is community work?

Dominelli has said of community work that it *has constituted a political activity through which ordinary people assert control over their communities and lives* (Dominelli,1990, p1). In line with a number of other writers she sees the activity of community work as being practised in a wide variety of ways. Popple (1995) has suggested that models of community intervention can range from community care to community action (pp54–73; see below for fuller discussion). The National Occupational Standards for Community Development describe community development as *a process that supports and promotes positive social change whilst challenging racism, poverty and marginalisation* (PAULO, 2002, p2).

Alison Gilchrist has suggested that community work:

> is fundamentally concerned with political processes, recognising that many of the problems experienced by people arise from political decisions about

financial priorities and power imbalances. Empowerment might be defined as increasing someone's ability (individually or collectively) to influence decisions which affect their lives . . . [the community worker must be prepared to] deal with potential conflicts and resistance to change . . . many decisions are . . . shrouded in the assumptions and prejudices of the policy makers, and manifest themselves as institutionalised discrimination. These need challenging through raising awareness, equality training and campaigning. The people in power must be re-educated to understand and respect the experiences and perspective of people who are oppressed. They must be compelled to take these views into account in the decision-making process. Or they must be replaced by those who can.

(Gilchrist, 1994, pp20–1)

Popple suggests that community workers:

can be at odds with the dominant ideology and . . . encouraging others to articulate their own discourse means that they do not fully agree with the dominant system. Therefore, it could be argued that community workers are strategic players in helping people make connections between their position and the need for change.

(1995, p98)

Gilchrist (1994) argues that this strategic approach involves community workers acting as change agents. She argues that community workers need to operate at three levels:

- **Dealing with psychological developments**   including consciousness – raising, developing empathetic relationships, challenging internalised oppression.

- **Practical arrangements**   change involves dealing with acquisition, allocation and management of resources. The key here is to ensure equal access. The community worker will therefore be seeking to develop a range of participation strategies including focusing on caring needs of those hoping to become involved.

- **Political processes**   which involves securing permanent changes in the allocation of resources from those with power to those without.

Freire, Fanon and Gramsci

Much of the more radical discourse around community work has been built around the work of two key thinkers: Paulo Freire and Antonio Gramsci. Mayo (1999) describes Freire as possessing *a vision of society as characterised by relations of power and domination* (p59). Among the key ideas we can take from Freire are the concepts of:

- Agency – *the ability of people to act in their own interests.*
- Democratic Education – *which is based on the idea of promoting education through dialogue, which will overcome the codification of reality which they experience. Central to this is the notion of praxis the linking together of action and reflection.*

- *Conscientizaçao (conscientisation) – 'education, as an exercise in freedom, is an act of knowing, a critical approach to reality'.*

(Mayo, 1999, p63)

Thompson also makes links to the Freirian notion of conscientization which he says is about:

- deindividualisation – *helping people understand the extent to which their position is a reflection of broader cultural and political patterns;*
- countering internalised oppression – *helping people overcome the feeling that they deserve their unequal position.*

This is a similar point to that made by Franz Fanon (1978), who, writing about the experience of Algerian people under French colonial rule, noted that colonisation impinges on the individuality of the colonised person and people. He argued that the colonised begin *to suffer from not being a white man [sic] to the degree that the white man [sic] imposes discrimination on me, makes me colonised . . . robs me of all individuality or worth* (Fanon, 1971, p98). This happens, he suggests, because the white, as coloniser, seeks to *frustrate the black, binding him [sic] with prohibitions of all kinds* (p175). The ruling white elite's political and economic power creates in the colonised black person a feeling of inferiority or 'dependency complex', which Fanon suggests is historically specific and related to the act of colonisation. This dependency is not, however, intrinsic, specific to a black identity, pathological. Rather, it is a consequence of relations of domination and power. Remove the domination, and the accompanying psychological and sexual stereotype dependent on it, and the dependency complex will itself be attenuated, removed.

These are important processes if human services practice is to be an emancipatory project, rather than a reinforcement of existing patterns of discrimination. We need to recognise that what services sometimes interpret as the passivity or lack of engagement of people who use services may be a reflection of the negative dominant power relationships which they experience on a day-to-day level. Replace those relationships of domination with a belief in the capacity of people to change their circumstances and we will see a significant change in the way in which people view their lives and their potential to change their circumstances.

Gramsci was an Italian Marxist who was active in establishing workers councils in Turin in the period during and after the end of the Second World War. He rejected what he believed was a simplistic version of Marxism which focused only on class relations and developed a broader conception of politics which drew attention to the struggle for moral and political leadership through a process he called *hegemony*. He maintained that ruling classes dominate through a mixture of force and consent where the consent is gained through assuming the political, moral and intellectual leadership in society. He argues that civil society (political parties, churches, cultural, charitable and voluntary groups) are central in maintaining hegemony. Civil society is the place where democratic struggles can be linked together. The ruling class maintains control by making their rule and the legitimacy of state rule appear like 'common sense'. It is then the role of external agents such as intellectuals, union organisers and community leaders to challenge this common sense. He believes that an oppressed group needs its own *organic intellectuals* (those that emerge from within their own ranks) to challenge these dominant ideas. He argues that:

> *'everyone' is a philosopher... it is not a question of introducing from scratch a scientific form of thought into everyone's individual life, but of renovating and making 'critical' an already existing activity.*
>
> (Gramsci, 1971, pp330–1, cited in Allman, 2001, p114)

Allman suggests that this passage should be read as Gramsci encouraging leaders or radical educators to help people *question their already existing activity (common-sense thinking) until it becomes 'critical' activity (dialectical thinking)* (Allman, 2001, p11). This focus on helping people become aware, to develop a critical understanding of the way their experiences are mediated by a wide range of social and economic factors, is central to Freire, Fanon and Gramsci and can become the key element of a new radical practice. To paraphrase Marx, philosophers may have described the world; the community worker's role is to change it.

ACTIVITY 3.3

Community work role play

You will need to divide into two groups for this role play. The scenario is based around an issue which has arisen within the local community. A group of people living in a high-rise block in Sanderstown, an area of social housing which scores high on all the indices of social deprivation and disadvantage – high levels of unemployment, low levels of educational attainment, poor health, lack of community facilities – has approached the local community worker at the neighbourhood community centre because they are concerned at the lack of facilities for young people in the area.

They have approached the local schools to ask them to increase their after-school provision but without any success. They have also approached the local councillor, who has dismissed them as unrepresentative and suggested that if there were any problems in the block he long ago resolved them. The local leisure services and youth departments are equally uncooperative.

Group A – As a community worker how would you deal with this problem? How would you help the local people formulate a strategy to resolve this problem?

Decide who will play the community worker and allocate key roles among the rest of the group. It is likely that you will be asking the local authority (LA) to attend a meeting to discuss your concerns. How would you plan for that meeting? Develop an agenda and work out your strategy for dealing with this meeting.

Group B – as representatives for the LA you realise you will have to meet with the residents. You are all confident that you have done everything in your power to sort out this estate's problems. It seems to you that this issue has been sparked by a number of people with their own agenda. How would you prepare for the meeting? Allocate roles within your group ensuring that all of the above interests are

ACTIVITY 3.3 *continued*

represented, such as housing management, leisure, youth, education, elected councillors, etc.

For both groups you realise that this issue may not be resolved in one meeting. How do you ensure that your strategy can work over time? How would you ensure that you maximise support for your views?

Comment

This activity is designed to be used within classroom settings. You may however adapt it so that it can be undertaken virtually by way of either chat rooms or through the use of VLEs. If you are looking at this scenario individually instead of role play map the activities of each group across the following matrix.

	Community group	Local authority
Strategy		
Identify key roles		
Organisation of own group		
Agenda		
Desired outcomes		

Within each box identify how each of the key actors – community group and local authority – would prepare for the meeting; organise themselves as a group; and how they would seek to develop their own agenda so that they achieved their desired outcomes. *You may wish to return to this exercise after reading Chapter 5 and see if your analysis changes in the light of the analysis in that chapter.*

Look at the National Occupational Standards outlined above and use the Community Work Skills Manual (Gilchrist, 1994). It is also worth looking at Taylor, M (2003).

What then of social work?

Lorenz (1994) suggested that social work faced many uncertainties but that *social work practice interprets and makes manifest the nature of solidarity that prevails in a particular society and the level of citizenship reached* (p10). Smale, Tuson, and Statham make a similar point when they suggest that 'social work is an integral part of the society within which it is practiced. It is one dimension of the way social problems are managed' (Smale,Tuson and Statham, 2000, p19).

Lyons (1999) has suggested that social work can be distinguished by its methodology: – field casework, group and community work and 'child rescue' services, *practices underpinned by concepts of concientisation and empowerment such as 'radical social work'*. To these can be added perspectives around identity or 'social division' such as feminism/ gender (Hanmer and Statham, 1999), disability (Campbell and Oliver,1996; Drake, 1999; Oliver and Sapey, 1999) and anti-racism (Ahmad, 1990; Aluffi-Pentini,

1996; Chouan *et al.*, 1996; Dominelli, 1997; Williams, Soydan and Johnson, 1998). Lorenz pointed to the challenge racism posed for the social professions when he suggested that:

> *Racism . . . represents a challenge to pedagogy as the institution responsible for society's cultural reproduction . . . It also provides a challenge to social work with its mainly unexamined notions of 'normality'.*
>
> (Lorenz, 1995, p34)

There have also been renewed calls for attention to be given to the impact and influence of users of services in the struggle to democratise and make relevant services and to reposition the user as a 'subject' (Williams, 1999) or an active agent in the process of social transformation (Beresford and Turner, 1997; Beresford *et al.*, 1999). Describing the exclusion of people in poverty from poverty discourse, Beresford and Croft (1995) argue that it is *only with their involvement that poverty discussion is likely to identify, reflect and advance their needs, concerns, interests* (p91). The same can be said to apply to users of welfare services and it will be a mark of social work's ability to promote social change how far it can create genuine partnerships with users and their organisations (see Chapter 5 for a fuller discussion of this issue).

One other factor is also worth remembering when we try to account for what social work is. In Shardlow and Payne's words, *social work is both a national and an international activity*. They raise the question of *how far the profession will continue to be defined through different national traditions and practices, or how far the future will see a harmonization of theory and practice across the various states* (Shardlow and Payne, 1997, p158). Johannesen (1997) has suggested that social work internationally is well placed to respond to the challenges posed by the UN's 1995 World Summit for social development in Copenhagen. He points to the way social work should target three particular commitments which emerged from the social summit – eradicating poverty, fighting unemployment and empowering disadvantaged groups (Johannesen, 1997, pp148–53). Lyons argues that the best way for social work to contribute to this process is through *taking a structural perspective and giving an increased emphasis to the concept of empowerment [which] clarifies the need to promote community networks and their interaction with the formal organizations in society* (Lyons, 1999, p46).

Giacinto and Lankshear (1998) suggest that social work is a fragmented and diffuse activity which is being increasingly eclipsed by trends in the delivery of welfare which promote the blurring of professional boundaries and the reduction of professional autonomy. The profession, they suggest, is riven with tensions, to the extent that it is not possible to speak of a 'Eurosocial work'. This appears to miss the point. Social work needs to be located within its own national and cultural contexts. However, that does not imply isolation because equally social work needs to learn from theory and practice in other countries (see Chapters 6 and 7 for an in-depth discussion of these issues).

Lorenz modelled the challenges facing social work as set out in Table 3.2

Table 3.2 The impact of globalisation

The impact of globalisation		
Risks		**Opportunities**
market-driven competition	**changing professional identities**	increased accountability
economic dictates suspend democratic policy-making	**sense of powerlessness**	new grassroots politics of community action
populism, politics of self-interest	**'end of grand political narratives'**	new international lobbies

Source: Lorenz,1998, p3

Aluffi-Pentini and Lorenz (1996) point to the importance of social professionals addressing racism when they describe the challenge faced by Italian youth and social workers who felt that *racism was a challenge to educators in all parts of the country, that all pedagogical interventions had to be embedded in a clear political analysis, that cultural differences reflected power differentials* (pvi). Dominelli clearly articulates the challenge for social work, which is to:

> *Contextualise social work within the state apparatus; understand the dynamics in both covert and overt forms of racism; recognise how racism is legitimated through social processes and institutions outside social work structures; and relate these to everyday routines in social work.*
> (Dominelli,1997, p19)

Humphries points to a further factor which impacts on the practice of social work – its relationship to people in poverty. As she suggests:

> *social work has always had a contradictory function in regulating the poor by both control and support. With growing state intervention in all aspects of social life comes a more direct inspectorial role for social workers…the tradition of emotional support is marginalized in the social worker's repertoire in a disciplinary society.*
> (Humphries,1997. p647)

Writing about the Irish child care system, Buckley, Skehill and O'Sullivan (1997) make a similar point when they refer to the way that *poor and disadvantaged people figure disproportionately in the child protection system* (p31). Barry argues that this is the key issue for social workers, who *operate at the interface of, and hence mediate between, advantage and disadvantage, self-determination and dependency, integration and marginalisation* (Barry, 1998, p7). Beresford and Wilson (1998) encapsulate the way in which social work can develop its role to tackle social exclusion. They argue that social work's focus on self-determination and empowerment demands that it develops participatory and inclusive ways of working with those who use services. This would suggest a way of linking together the concerns of both professions. How can this be achieved?

Coming together – new professional identities?

Social and community work can now be seen to share some common knowledge, skills and values. These may include those listed in Table 3.3.

Table 3. 3 Knowledge base of community work and social work

Knowledge	Community work	Social work
Theoretical paradigm	Sociology/politics	Sociology/psychology
Theoretical paradigm	Social policy	Social policy
Practice framework	Law and policy analysis	Law and policy framework
Action perspective	Networking and community action	Networking
Action perspective	Partnership and power	Partnership and cooperation
Primary focus	International/national	National/international

Table 3.3 illustrates the points of similarity between the two professional activities, while at the same time identifying subtle differences of emphasis which locate the activities of both professions within different elements of the welfare state. While they share theoretical concerns with sociology and social policy, they in turn look to other theoretical disciplines for their identity. Community work is concerned much more explicitly with challenging power at a political level and so looks to politics to sharpen its understanding of the way social change can be brought about. The concern noted above with the work of Gramsci and Freire is a clear illustration of this process (Ledwith, 1997; Mayo, 1999; Allman, 200). Social work looks to psychology to reflect its concern with the individual and with the necessity of engaging with internal psychological processes of change (Pinkney, 1999; Kendall, 2000).

While both professions work within clearly defined legal frameworks, community work's concern is more with using the law as a tool to challenge the actions of political actors at local and national levels (Law Centres Federation, 2001; Bateman, 2006). Social work is more concerned with the procedural elements of law and to the extent to which the law is used to challenge the decisions of public bodies, it is frequently used to support individual rather than collective rights (Brayne and Carr, 2005).

The action perspective of both professions is also different. Community work's focus is on engaging with networks to secure change at community, neighbourhood or regional levels. Often this will involve pursuing strategies of community action which seek to mobilise people to secure long-term change (Popple, 1995; Hoggett, 1997). To social workers networking often means developing relationships with other professions operating in the same locality. It often infers the need for better coordination of service delivery and closer collaboration between professions working in the same field (Overtriet, 1997; Coulshed and Mullender, 2001; Quinney, 2006). Finally, while both professions share a commitment to international work, the focus within the community work literature is much more on learning from other countries (Community Development Journal, 1990 to present; Craig and Mayo, 1994). Within social work a concern with international issues is increasingly important but is secondary to the focus on practice within the UK (Adams, Dominelli and Payne, 2005; Hatton, 2006; Lyons and Lawrence, 2006).

Sharing values

Table 3.4 Common values?

Values	Community work	Social work
Tackling discrimination	ADP/AOP	ADP/AOP
Beyond discrimination	Focus on diversity and equality	Focus on diversity
Tackling change	Empowerment/advocacy	Empowerment/advocacy
Primary value	Collectivisation	Individualisation
New *v* old?	Organisational innovation	Organisational change

As can be seen in Table 3.4, there are significant points of connection between the values underpinning social and community work. Both have a central concern with discrimination and oppression (Harris, 1994; Gil, 1998; Thompson, 2001) and with developing strategies to overcome them. These strategies may differ slightly, focusing on individual, achievable goals (social work) or longer, more strategic change (community work) but this commitment is central to good practice across both sets of professional activity (see discussion of key roles above).

Community work may have a greater focus on the pursuit of equality but both share a concern with developing work in a way which promotes diversity and difference. Both share concerns with empowerment and advocacy (see Chapter 2) and with organisational as well as individual change. Community work's focus may, however, be with promoting new organisational structures which generate participation and control such as collective working, parity and community control (Law Centres Federation, 2001). Social work's focus is more often on effective service delivery, quality enhancement and strategic leadership (Coulshed and Mullender, 2001).

The principles shared across the two professions can be most usefully articulated through Table 3.5.

Table 3.5 Principles which are shared by community and social work

Principle	Community work (drawn from Pringle, 1995; Ife, 1999)	Social work
Confront structural disadvantage	To be consistent with a social justice perspective needs to ensure that it does not reinforce oppression/discrimination, that community worker is aware of own prejudices/ assumptions and of the complex way class, race, gender, etc., interact	Enhance focus on individual with recognition of way people who use services are impacted upon by wider structural and cultural factors (Thompson, 1997; Gill, 2001; Dalrymple and Burke, 2006)
Human rights	Important in two senses – the negative (protection of human rights) and positive (the promotion of human rights)	Promotes idea of protecting people using services by matching HRs against current policy (Brayne and Carr 2005)

Empowerment	'Providing people with the resources, opportunities, knowledge and skills to increase the capacity to determine their own future, and to participate in and affect the life of the community' (Ife, p182)	Challenges power relationships and promotes individual and collective empowerment, but sometimes constrained by regulatory framework (Baistow,1994)
Self-reliance	Community should seek to utilise its own resources rather than relying on external support, this not achievable in total but aim should be to maximise, e.g. LETS schemes, also has elements of social enterprise – Chapter 4	Need to avoid danger of pathologising service users/carers and instead promote their self-activity and empowerment (see discussion of community work above)
Immediate goals and ultimate visions	Essential to maintain balance between the immediate and the long term, both indispensable to each other	Focus on crisis intervention can render long-term goals invisible
The pace of development	CD is by its nature a long-term process, change occurs at the community's own pace	Replace short-termism such as task-centred social work, brief solution-focused therapy with longer-term perspective which focuses on social change
Community building	'Involves strengthening the social interactions within the community, bringing people together, and helping them communicate with each other in a way that can lead to genuine dialogue, understanding and social action' (Ife, p191)	Need to de-individualise social problems (Freire, 1972; Thompson, 1997)
Process and outcome	The process itself is important in determining the outcome, but need to keep in mind both and that both are integrated	Return to preventative work rather than crisis intervention
Inclusiveness	Based on dialogue, understanding, respect for other person's point of view even if it is different, always be ready to learn from others, 'the essence of non-violence is to oppose structures and ideas, but not people' (Ife, p195)	Promote greater level of service user involvement – move beyond tokenism – see Chapter 5
External expertise	Be deeply distrustful of any solution imposed from outside; external experts need to value the contribution of local communities	Desire for professionalism should not create expectation of social worker as 'expert' whose knowledge and skills becomes privileged over non-qualified staff and service users and carers
Participation	Aims to maximise participation while recognising that different people have different skills, broadens participation and values all	Participation should become part of wider strategy which not only involves service users but also leads social workers to question own role in their organisations and seek to democratise those organisations

Defining need	Encouraging communities to articulate needs and then act so that they can be met	Encouraging service users/carers to articulate own needs

---

CASE STUDY

Article One – an Intercultural youth work project in the Netherlands

This project is based in Helmond, a city near Eindhoven. It provides a small insight into how the concerns of social workers and community workers can be reflected in one project. The project title is taken from Article One of the Dutch Constitution which says that:

> *All inhabitants of the Netherlands will be treated equally in equal situations. There shall be no discrimination on the grounds of religion, philosophy of life, political orientation, race, gender or any other grounds.*

This is an inter-agency project which works towards civil and human rights and against racism. The development of identity plays a key role in the group's work. It is seen as a continuous process of enclosure and exclusion, which are defined as, enclosure – the process of becoming associated with others who are alike *and* exclusion – the emotional and cognitive distancing from other groups that are 'different'.

Both processes are important to create one's identity. Hoffman and Maduro suggest that:

> *the problem of racism arises when the differences become fixed, when it becomes 'natural', self evident, and common sense that your group is more sophisticated and intelligent and has achieved more than certain other groups. Preventative anti-racism must therefore engage in the process of identity formation and free itself from a notion of fixed identities.*
>
> (1996, p136)

They suggest that the current multicultural environment offers a rich variety of lifestyles for young people to choose and that consequently an intercultural education needs to be developed to assist young people make appropriate choices. They argue for the idea of intercultural education as taking responsibility *(p143).*

They suggest two principles for intercultural education:

1. *The principle of* inclusive thinking, or non-exclusion: all participants in the learning process have equal access to learning opportunities and should not be obstructed by categories constructed by others on the grounds of race, sex, culture or class.

2. *The principle that* all interaction has to respect the uniqueness of each individual. *This means that all educational methods, as well as social policies and other organisational arrangements, need to be measured against this criteria.*

The work of Article One suggests ways in which social workers, pedagogues (see Chapter 6) and community development workers can begin to tackle the racism they encounter. They suggest that our role as change agents who promote processes of social transformation is both appropriate and necessary if we are to practise in ways which are anti-discriminatory and anti-oppressive.

A framework for understanding social and community work

How then can we begin to make sense of the similarities and differences within these two apparently distinct approaches? This section will examine these issues within a framework which draws on theoretical and practical issues from both traditions. To do this it is necessary to conceptualise the debate as representing both a continuum from the individual to the structural and an iterative dialogue between the different levels which represents a properly reflexive account of how the different traditions operate. This may sound overly complex but is in fact a relatively simple process as demonstrated by Figures 3.1 and 3.2 and the discussion below.

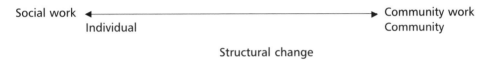

Social work   Community work
Individual   Community

Structural change

Figure 3.1 The continuum between social and community work

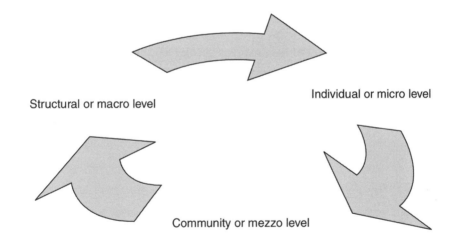

Structural or macro level

Individual or micro level

Community or mezzo level

Figure 3.2 The interaction between social and community work

The individual or micro level

Figures 3.1 and 3.2 provide a way of visualising the connections between social and community work. The continuum reflects the belief that the professional activities are a substantial distance apart. It posits a view of social work as being about individual change and community work as being about structural change. They may share some common concerns within local communities but their foci and rationale are different. The second diagram, however, suggests that the process of interaction between the individual and the structural is much more continuous, reflective and that it constitutes a process in movement. This more clearly reflects the dynamic interplay which, this book suggests, is the basis of good practice.

Clearly neither social nor community work has legitimacy unless their primary focus is seen as improving the life chances of the most marginalised and excluded sections of society. The International Federation of Social Workers and the International Association of Schools of Social Work agreed at a Joint Congress in Montreal in July 2000 the following definition of social work:

> *The social work profession promotes social change, problem solving in human relationships and the empowerment and liberation of people to enhance well-being. Utilising theories of human behaviour and social systems, social work intervenes at the points where people interact with their environments; principles of human rights and social justice are fundamental to social work.*
>
> (www.ifsw.org.uk, quoted in Lyons and Lawrence, 2006, p6)

Dominelli (2004) has argued that to understand the service user experience at the local level we need to focus on the power relationship between the service user and worker (Hugman, 1992; Hatton and Nugent, 1993; Adams, 2001). However, following Foucault, Dominelli sees power as not just a zero-sum game (A has power over B, B can only change this by taking power from A) but as an interactional process that *creates positive environments for communication and action and which can result in win–win situations* (p41). In this sense no one individual (or indeed group) can be *either totally powerful or powerless* (Dominelli, 2004, p41). This position allows us to see people as not just objects who are acted upon by external powerful forces but as being capable of resistance and the creation of new realities over which they can exercise control. For social workers this means seeing beyond the service user as someone whose experience is framed only by their relationship to the service they use. It involves seeing them also as active agents of change themselves. For community workers this means not defining people within the communities within which they work as being downtrodden, exploited or marginalised but instead seeing them as the people who can, through their own skills and resourcefulness, generate change themselves.

The mezzo or group level

Writing about homelessness, Avramov described the mezzo level as being the arena in which we can map the intermediate causes of the problems people face. He suggests that analysis at this level can tell us about:

> *The ways in which families, friends, informal networks, neighbourhoods, peer groups and sub-cultural groups operate and how they may be preventing or exacerbating (housing) exclusion.*
>
> (Avramov, 1997, p21)

This may seem a more appropriate level of intervention for community rather than social workers. Community work is largely about building and sustaining networks, relating to peer groups and tackling exclusion (Gilchrist, 1994; Popple, 1995). However, social work must also have a role in what Parton and O'Byrne (2000) call the 'art of resistance', which is based on the belief that, *people, no matter what their circumstances, have significant resources within and around them... social workers... can help people refocus their resources to assist them best in accomplishing their goals* (p184). This is a particular challenge for social work because of the way many service users are presented as being responsible for the position they find themselves in. Young people are increasingly criminalised through ASBOs and the demonisation of elements of youth culture (such as Hoodies, etc.). Jordan (2000) has pointed to the way social work is asked to buy into a discourse of service users as problematic and being unable to relate to the broader society. The people we work with as social workers or community workers are often pathologised and seen as dysfunctional and a 'threat' to normal society. As he notes:

> *Service users react negatively to what they perceive as attempts to blame them for their problems, and to attribute causation to their character, personality, attitudes or motivation, pathologizing their behaviour and locating all their difficulties in themselves... [they] are expert in rejecting these discourses of stigma and dysfunction and in developing their own narratives of injustice, oppression and exclusion, identifying the external forces in the economy and polity which disadvantage and trap them.*
>
> (Jordan, 2000, p216)

Social workers and community workers can therefore both be seen to have a role in promoting these positive models of the individuals and communities with which they work. They can begin to secure changes which challenge the social construction of the service user as dependent and deficient and which are legitimised through 'common sense' understandings of users of services as 'other', 'different' and 'deficient'.

Macro or structural work

This approach is more often associated with community work, although writers such as Thompson (2001), Mullally (1997), Fook (2000) and Brueggemann (2006) all suggest the importance of social workers looking at the structural or macro level, if they want to secure lasting and sustainable social change. Indeed both Mullaly and Brueggemann's work focuses heavily on what are often assumed to be community work strategies. Brueggemann describes macro-social work as *the practice of helping individuals and groups solve social problems and make social change at the community, organizational, societal, and global levels* (Brueggemann, 2006, p7). Pierson suggests that social workers should see their role as a *catalyst and change agent regardless of your position in the organisation* (Pierson, 2002, p232). Pierson's focus is on tackling social exclusion. Barry makes a similar point when she says:

> *Social work in its task of meeting human need and developing human potential and resources, must, therefore, inevitably address problems associated with social exclusion and, at least, ensure that the services provided – or the terms on which they are made available – do not further marginalize the already excluded.*
>
> (Barry, 1998, p8).

At a time when levels of social inequality are deepening (Gordon and Townsend, 2000; Darton and Streliz, 2003; Palmer, Carr and Kenway, 2004), community is increasingly being seen as a potential site through which meaningful change can occur. Sometimes this is reflected in the more conservative attempts to reconstitute community such as communitarianism, with its focus on rights and responsibilities (normally the latter – see Tan,1998 and Jordan, 2000; see Chapter 4). Jordan (2000) suggests a role for social work in the community as being to *soften the harshness of the informal code, to uphold the rights of the oppressed within all social units, and to develop more constructive links with the world outside* (p200).

To move forward in this way social and community work need a perspective which fuses together advocacy and empowerment. We will look at how this can be achieved in Chapter 4.

ACTIVITY 3.4

Perspectives of Irish women community activists

Below are comments from women the author interviewed during research in Ireland. Their comments reflect some of the dilemmas faced by people active in the community when they try to articulate their desires and aspirations. Answer the following questions.

- *As a social worker, how would you work with these women to support their aspirations for change?*

- *As a community worker, how would you work with these women to support their aspirations for change?*

- *Would there be any differences in the approaches you adopted? If so what would they be?*

> *We are all working-class women, the majority early school leavers, we are all disadvantaged in relation to education and training. We recognised we all have value and all have something to offer and we were all very active before the funding . . . in communities, throughout disadvantaged areas. [They designed courses aimed at working-class women who they felt needed a progression route into higher education.]*

> *Women have been treated as second-class citizens, for generations men have been seen to speak more assertively on things . . . a lot of poorer women seem to be passive because they have not got the energy for all this fight, they are worrying about the day-to-day survival and the struggles. While I can understand that I feel that if they remain in the victim syndrome things will never change. I'm not a victim, I'm a survivor.*

> *I think Travelling working-class women are doubly marginalised . . . because they have to struggle with being working class and poor as well as being a Traveller . . . it's harder for them in the society we have today because they are just ostracised completely from communities. They are not allowed to use public houses, cinemas, they are victimised an awful lot.*

ACTIVITY **3.4** *continued*

I'm part of a women's group where we do our own research, we produce our own books, we access our own funding. It's like because we are working class you can't manage monies and yet we get more from our small amount of funding and we are doing more with it for people on the ground than [others] are with [their] millions.

(Comments drawn from interviews with women in Cork, Ireland, which the author conducted as part of comparative research into community work in Ireland, Denmark and the UK.)

Comment

These quotations reflect a number of the key issues highlighted in the chapter. Read them carefully and see how they relate to the National Occupational Standards and the values and principles articulated in this chapter.

C H A P T E R   S U M M A R Y

This chapter has looked at the contribution that both social and community work can make to help us become effective and critical practitioners. It suggests continuities in our practice which can allow us to move beyond the dichotomies of 'social work equals individualised' approaches and 'community work provides the more collective, radical alternative'. It demonstrates the connectedness of both forms of practice but builds on the analysis in Chapter 2 to suggest that we can develop an integrated form of practice which can allow us to intervene at micro, mezzo and macro levels.

FURTHER READING

Bauman, Z (2001) *Community – seeking safety in an insecure world*. Cambridge: Polity Press.
A good discussion of the way in which the concept of community has been used and misused.

Harris, A (1994) *Community work skills manual*. Newcastle: Association of Community Workers.
A handbook which focuses on the actual activities undertaken by community workers and provides a short explanation of how issues such as power impact on community work practice.

Hoggett, P (ed.) (1997) *Contested communities: experiences, struggles, policies*. Bristol: Policy Press.
A collection which looks at the way communities have actively sought to resist the impact of negative social and economic changes.

Ife, J (1999) *Community development: creating community alternatives – vision, analysis and practice.* Sydney: Longman Pearson.
A clear, well-written account of the principles of community development practice. Ife is an Australian writer but draws on a wide range of material which is relevant to UK social and community work.

WEBSITES

Federation for Community Development Learning **www.fcdl-org.uk**

ESRC Research Centre for Analysis of Social Exclusion (CASE) **http://sticerd.lse.ac.uk/case/**

Joseph Rowntree Foundation Research Findings **www.jrf.org.uk/knowledge/findings/**

Chapter 4

The voluntary and independent sectors: Communitarianism, compact or conflict?

A C H I E V I N G   A   S O C I A L   W O R K   D E G R E E

This chapter will help you begin to meet the following National Occupational Standards for social work.

Key Role 1: Prepare for and work with individuals, families, carers, groups and communities to assess their needs and circumstances.
- Work with individuals, families, carers, groups and communities to enable them to analyse, identify, clarify and express their strengths, expectations and limitations.
- Work with individuals, families, carers, groups and communities to enable them to assess and make informed decisions about their needs, circumstances, risks, preferred options and resources.

Key Role 2: Plan, carry out, review and evaluate social work practice, with individuals, families, carers, groups, communities and other professionals.
- Develop and maintain relationships with individuals, families, carers, groups, communities and others.
- Help groups to achieve planned outcomes for their members and to evaluate the appropriateness of their work.

Key Role 3: Support individuals to represent their needs, views and circumstances.
- Advocate for, and with individuals, families, carers, groups and communities.
- Work with individuals, families, carers, groups and communities to select the best form of representation for decision-making forums.
- Enable individuals, families, carers, groups and communities to be involved in decision-making forums.

Key Role 4: Manage risk to individuals, families, carers, groups and communities.
- Balance the rights and responsibilities of individuals, families, carers, groups and communities with associated risk.

Key Role 5: Manage and be accountable, with supervision and support for your own social work practice within your organisation.
- Carry out duties using accountable professional judgement and knowledge-based social work practice.
- Contribute to monitoring the quality of the services provided
- Share records with individuals, families, carers, groups and communities.
- Work within multi-disciplinary and multi-organisational teams, networks and systems.
- Deal constructively with disagreements and conflict within relationships.

Key Role 6: Demonstrate professional competence in social work practice.
- Work within the principles and values underpinning social work practice.
- Devise strategies to deal with ethical issues, dilemmas and conflicts.
- Contribute to policy review and development.

Achieving a Community Work qualification

This chapter will also begin to help you achieve the National Occupational Standards in Community Development.

National Occupational standards in Community Development

Key Role A: Develop working relationships with communities and organisations.

Key Role B:	*Encourage people to work with and learn from each other.*
Key Role C:	*Work with people in communities to plan for change and take collective action.*
Key Role D:	*Work with people in communities to develop and use frameworks for evaluation.*
Key Role E:	*Develop community organisations.*
Key Role F:	*Reflect and develop own practice role.*

(PAULO, 2002 National Occupational Standards in Community Development Work, **www.fcdl.org.uk/ publications/documents/nos/standards**, retrieved 5 July 2006)

Introduction

The more radical discourses around community work featured in earlier chapters not surprisingly differ in style, emphasis and philosophy from those put forward by government, particularly the successive Conservative governments from 1979 to 1997 which placed an emphasis on community responsibility through ideas such as Neighbourhood Watch or 'active citizenship'. Often such conceptions evoked, uncritically, nostalgic notions of the past such as Victorian conceptions of frugality, family responsibility and minimum state intervention. The family was envisioned as the fulcrum of social life. New Labour when it came to power in 1997 sought to distance itself from such analysis by promoting a more inclusive sense of community. Some writers have seen this attempt to recraft the idea of community as a 'fundamental concept' in New Labour's ideology (Fremeaux, 2005, p267). Drawing on Gidden's ideas about the 'Third Way' (the alternative to the politics of the left or right), New Labour promoted an idea of community which offered an alternative to centralised and top-down policies and which attempted to invoke the capacity of the community to revitalise and regenerate local areas (Fremeaux, 2005).

This approach is exemplified in programmes such as New Deal for Communities, Single Regeneration Partnerships and the compact between the government and the voluntary sector. At the heart of this concern, however, is a process in which the needs of the community and the individual become elided. Community can then be promoted in an unproblematic and uncritical way so that the interests of the community become the interests of all (see Chapter 3; Jordan, 1996; Fremeaux, 2005). As Fremeaux points out, Tony Blair saw the community as the *collective ability to further the individual's interests* (Blair, 1994, quoted in Fremeaux, 2005, p270). At the heart of this confusion over the nature of community is New Labour's articulation of the philosophy of communitarianism, which is discussed below.

The reconfiguration of welfare which characterised both the Conservative administration between 1979 and 1997 and New Labour since 1997 has been predicated on the ideological assumption that the state creates dependency, stifles initiative and is intrinsically a poor way of delivering welfare. The result has been the creation, or more accurately the enshrining, of what has been variously known as a 'mixed economy of welfare' (Johnson,1999), 'welfare pluralism' (Gould, 1993) or the establishment of 'quasi-markets in welfare' (Le Grand, 1991).

The mixed economy of welfare, Johnson (1999) suggests, is defined by the presence of four sectors in the production and delivery of welfare: the state sector; the commercial sector; the voluntary (non-profit or third) sector; the informal sector (family, friends and neighbours). These sectors have, he argues, always been present; the key factor which distinguishes welfare states is the balance between them. This in turn varies along four dimensions: between countries, between historical periods, between services and between one component of a service and another (for example, the degree of privatisation, role of the voluntary sector) (Johnson, 1999, p22–9).

Gould suggests that these developments can be traced back to the 1980s and he argues that:

> The more affluent members of the working class were coming to resent the burden of taxation to finance a welfare state from which there seemed to be few marginal gains for them. Employers, coping with recession and the threat of increased competition from the countries of the Pacific Rim, such as Japan, wanted a reduction in the size of the public sectors. Growing sections of the middle class, particularly those employed in the private sector, were also demanding that welfare spending be reduced.
>
> (Gould, 1993, p7)

Ginsburg (1992) has pointed out how the insecure nature of the welfare state in capitalist societies limits their scope to alleviate or mitigate hardship. As a consequence *the overall impact of the welfare state under capitalism on the social class distribution of welfare has been to stabilise and thus reinforce the class structure* (p4). These processes lead to a situation in which the legitimacy of the welfare state is often jeopardised by crises in the economy. This legitimacy can be challenged because it is seen to inhibit productivity, reduce innovation and create dependency. People will have no motivation for moving beyond their situation because the welfare safety net will ensure that they are always provided for. Indeed, proponents of welfare pluralism from the radical right see the welfare state as being more about the protection of the interests of those who work within it (Stoesz and Midgely, 1991).

A consequence of these trends was, Clarke, Langan and Williams (2001) assert, the development of a welfare pluralism which has four main features.

* Welfare services have been broken up and/or become fragmented so that rather than a welfare state which reflected a common set of assumptions and concerns we now have a welfare state which is provided through an array of public, private and voluntary sector organisations. Significantly this has led to demands that the voluntary sector should play a more substantial role in welfare provision (see later in this chapter for the way in which this trend has developed).

* The rise of consumerism – the belief that welfare is best delivered through the market and that the market will ensure the most efficient use of welfare resources.

* New regimes of inspection and regulation (see Chapter 1) based on a belief that the provider of services should be separated from the purchaser of services to the extent that *the 1990s saw a significant expansion of regulatory, inspection*

and audit agencies, offering new means for control 'at arm's length' (Clarke, Langan and Williams, 2001, p88).

- The transfer of responsibilities from the public to the private realm, particularly the family. Prior to 1997 this was seen as a justifiable attempt to remove the state from interference in the family. Fox Harding (1997) has linked these arguments to those of the radical right (although she also demonstrates how some on the left also buy into this approach) when she says that:

> *freedom from state control is stressed; the state is seen as threatening, as a force to be kept within bounds; and counterweights to state power are highly valued. The family may be seen as a locus of alternative power. It is also seen as a locus of social responsibility.*
>
> (p22)

Since 1997 there has been some recognition that this can lead to gendered forms of care. While there has been some recognition of the 'costs' of informal care on families (Carers Recognition Act, and child care allowances), there has also been an attempt to 'problematise' certain families, particularly those suffering exclusion or marginalisation, through an increased emphasis on anti-social behaviour, inadequate parenting (Jordan, 2002).

Communitarianism

Concern about the pathologising of the poor, which lay at the heart of American debates on the underclass (see Chapter 1), led a group of liberal academics to attempt to restate a social philosophy which recognised the way people's lives were influenced by the network of social arrangements within the locality. Etzioni, a leading proponent of communitarianism claimed that their agenda was predicated on the need to *bring about the changes in values, habits and public policy that will allow us to do for society what the environmental movement does for nature; to safeguard and enhance our future* (Etzioni, 1993, p3).

The communitarian philosophy was based on the need to rekindle people's sense of social responsibility by correcting the 'imbalance' between citizens' rights and responsibilities. Etzioni argued that this could best be achieved by a four-fold strategy which included:

- *a moratorium on the development of new rights;*
- *a re-establishment of the link between rights and responsibilities;*
- *the recognition that 'some responsibilities do not entail rights';*
- *the adjustment of some rights to changing circumstances.*

(Etzioni, 1993, pp263–4)

He argues that at the heart of their social philosophy lies the idea of 'reciprocity', the notion that *each member of society owes something to all the rest, and the community owes something to its members...members of the community have a responsibility to the greatest extent to provide for themselves and their families* (p263–4).

This framework suggests a view of people as one in which *individuals cannot be perceived to exist in a vacuum. Individuals are an inherent part of their community* (Mullard and Spicker, 1998, p200). Mullard and Spicker point to the way in which the apparent inclusiveness of communitarianism can mask potential discrimination in that it can offer:

> preference to some people over others. The social relationships of family and community imply that people have special responsibilities to the people they are closest to, responsibilities which go over and above the responsibilities they have to others.
>
> (p95)

Perversely then, communitarianism could further the processes of social exclusion which New Labour has sought to tackle through its social policies, particularly through the project teams set up to tackle social exclusion which were initially based in the Cabinet Office and more recently in the Office of the Deputy Prime Minister. Before we deal with this argument it is worth noting the important way in which communitarian ideas have influenced New Labour's social policy agenda. Commenting on the development of New Labour's social philosophy, Ruth Lister pointed out how:

> When Tony Blair talks the language of citizenship, it is to emphasise obligations and responsibilities. This is reflected in the statement of values that replaced Clause 4 of the party's constitution. This offers the ideal of a 'community…where the rights we enjoy reflect the duties we owe,'
> …Gordon Brown, announcing his 'new deal' on youth unemployment
> …promised that 'opportunities and responsibilities' would dominate Labour's modernisation of the welfare state.
>
> (Lister, 1998, p49)

Johnson (1999) suggests that *communitarianism has implications for policy which go well beyond the personal social services and community care, but it has a particular significance in this area* (p92). He suggests that it is particularly resonant in debates concerning decentralisation with its implied increased role for local agencies and its emphasis on community as the unit of social organisation. He argues, however, that communitarians, although they would welcome the increased emphasis on self-reliance and mutual aid, would probably baulk at the idea of such groupings becoming campaigning or advocacy organisations. Johnson suggests that New Labour would be supportive of such developments because they have *constantly emphasised the empowerment of users and carers* (p93) with its focus on the idea of welfare recipients as consumers or even stakeholders in society. This is at best debatable as New Labour has not been sympathetic to radical campaigning activity. As Popple and Redmond point out:

> Now radical work can be quickly identified and isolated, funding can be withdrawn on the back of regular assessment of project work, and reassigned to 'safe' and often competing projects.
>
> (Popple and Redmond, 2000, p396)

Jordan suggests that an emphasis on choice and the user as consumer typifies the way the welfare state is developing. He argues that:

> The public infrastructure is redesigned so as to promote choice, giving citizens information (for instance in the form of league tables) about the performance of hospitals, school and care homes, so that they can switch to the best amenities.
>
> (Jordan, 2006, p142)

However, as he suggests, those without the material resources to make these choices real lose out in this newly marketised form of welfare.

The community may then only meet the needs of a section of society, one which buys into the welfare pluralism we have discussed earlier. What then becomes of those who are not part of this grouping – those who are excluded or marginalised – and who are often the focus of social work intervention? It is helpful here to return to the discussion of social exclusion in chapter 2. Silver notes that by the mid-1980s social exclusion had come to represent a wider understanding of social problems:

> The term referred not only to the rise in long-term and recurrent unemployment, but also to the growing instability of social bonds: family instability, single-member households, social isolation, and the decline of class solidarity based on unions, the labour market, and the working-class neighbourhood and social networks. There were not only material but also spiritual and symbolic aspects to this phenomenon.
>
> (Silver, 1994, p533)

Spicker (1995) suggests that the French concern has been to foster a sense of *mutualité* or solidarity as exemplified by the development of the *Revenu Minimum d'Insertion*, a benefit established as a safety net for those without other entitlements and which *seeks to draw people into defined relationships with the rest of society* (p9).

The European Commission's final report of the Poverty 3 programme in 1995 noted that the concept of social exclusion was gradually replacing poverty as the operative concept in member states and at community level. The report said of social exclusion that:

> We are acknowledging that the problem is no longer one of inequity between the top and bottom of the scale (up/down) but also one of the distance within society between those who are active members and those who are forced towards the fringes (in/out). We are also highlighting the effects of the way society is developing and the concomitant risk of social disintegration and, finally we are affirming that for both the persons concerned and society itself, this is a process of change and not a set of fixed and static situations...
> ... there is not only one group – and a small one at that – of people living in permanent poverty and exclusion but a variety of – increasingly large – groups whose economic and social integration is insecure, who experience periods of sporadic or recurrent poverty and who are threatened by the loss of social ties which accompanies the process of social exclusion.
>
> (European Commission, 1995, p7)

65

As we noted earlier, Levitas (1998) suggests three distinct discourses around social exclusion which she characterises as the redistributive discourse, the moral underclass discourse and the social integrationist discourse. Drawing on Levitas' analysis we can codify these discourses and attempt to suggest how they can 'fit' with our conceptualisation of welfare states.

These concepts of the underclass, social exclusion and communitarianism, when related to discourses around the family which engage more with ideas of 'blame' rather than rights, have led to an important resonance within social work as they characterise the people with whom we work in ways which have direct implications for social work interventions. As Jordan (2002) suggests, Labour's distrust and dislike of public services can lead to:

> A very restricted view of social work's role . . . suspicion of the public sector, and its top down notions of implementation . . . social welfare services need to recapture their sense of moral purpose, as transformative agencies that thrive on change and uncertainty, rather than as structural features in a system of regulation and control.
>
> (pp218–19)

This move from neo-liberalism to communitarianism was predicated on an interchange of ideological positions between neo-liberal and communitarian ideals which led to a focus on delivering welfare outside of state institutions.

Implications for social work

This discussion of the way the nature of the welfare state has changed has clear implications for the practice of social work. It suggests that attempts to characterise social work as an activity which takes place in the statutory sector can provide an inaccurate account of the way social work is heading. While qualified social workers still tend to gravitate toward working in local authorities, whether in the children or adult workforce or multi-disciplinary initiatives such as Youth Offending Teams or Community Mental Health teams, much of the more innovative practice is taking place outside these sectors and can be found in the voluntary and independent sectors (see Took, 2005). Indeed, the importance of community involvement in local governance is a factor which is being recognised as increasingly important (Maguire and Truscott, 2006).

Morison (2000) saw evidence of an *increasing involvement by the voluntary sector in delivering a whole range of services* (p105). He noted how the voluntary sector had been estimated to account for 1 in 25 of the workforce, with a total contribution to the economy of £25 billion per annum. Clearly the sector is not therefore an insignificant part of the welfare environment in the UK. Bateman has recently drawn attention to how important the voluntary sector is, for instance, on the development of welfare advice services (Bateman, 2006).

Popple and Redmond (2000) suggested that involvement with the voluntary sector was one way in which New Labour could be seen to distance itself from the policies of the previous Conservative administration. However, as they noted, the motivation for such developments was not always based on altruism but instead was conditioned by the fact that:

> *The voluntary sector delivers a range of services cheaper than those in the state or provided for by the private sector, not least because such agencies are long used to operating with fewer overheads, in accommodation that is usually cheaper, and of a lower standard than that found in the public sector. Here, staff often female, are paid less and employed on short term contracts.*
> (Popple and Redmond, 2000, p397)

Whatever the motivation, it is undoubtedly true that the voluntary sector has been given a pivotal role in delivering social work and welfare services. The compact between the government and the voluntary sector agreed in 1998 gave formal expression to this improved relationship, although to what extent it has allowed the voluntary sector to become the lead sector is debatable. The aims of the compact were *the creation of a new approach to partnerships between the statutory and voluntary and community sectors – an approach which is of mutual advantage based on shared values and mutual respect* (Carrington, 2002, p2). The aim was to make these principles a key part of the local infrastructure and day-to-day activities. This was coupled with a commitment to a more stable funding regime, including the award of three-year contracts instead of the previous one-year contracts. Osborne and McLaughlin (2002, p61) suggest that the compact can provide:

> *potential participative challenges to its concept of representative democracy ... and real dangers to the voluntary sector, which could lead to the negation of its legitimate societal roles as independent watchdog and voice for the marginalised and oppressed.*

Osborne and McLaughlin suggest that for positive rather than negative outcomes to be achieved a number of key factors must be in place.

- The partnerships involved should be locally owned rather than centrally imposed.
- Both sides need to develop relationships based on trust.
- The process should be led by the voluntary sector.
- The replacement of hierarchical forms of control with local control.
- Voluntary organisations should be involved in developing policy, not just implementing it.
- The process should embrace the large range of community organisations and community interests not just the traditional voluntary sector.

Certainly the support the government has shown for the voluntary sector centres much more on the services it delivers than any increased capacity to challenge or pursue a radical agenda over the structures and the overall development of services, which it was suggested (in the previous chapter) should be part of any realignment of social work to allow it to pursue a social change agenda.

This increasing role can come at a price. Wyatt (2002) argues that when the state seeks to draw voluntary organisations into partnership the result can be that they become peripheral, particularly where provision is patchy and discontinuous. The result may be that the vibrancy and diversity of the sector may be diminished as local or national government seeks to standardise relationships. As he argues:

> *The importance and strength of voluntary organisations taken together is that they express the right and willingness of citizens to do what they want, in the way that they want, for the benefit of themselves and others. The resulting diversity and non-conformity open up possibilities of change, of challenge, of offering alternatives, and doing something better. The right to be different is protected but also increasingly restricted by regulation from the government sphere.*
>
> (Wyatt, 2002, p177)

The result, he suggests, is that voluntary organisations may be sucked further *into the sphere of government interest* (p178) and end up being co-opted by the state.

ACTIVITY 4.1

Implications for social and community work
Using the analysis of the three approaches to welfare provision discussed above – the underclass, communitarianism and social exclusion – use the internet to find three voluntary organisations, one national, one which covers a city/town and one of a small local organisation. How would you evaluate their activity against the approaches and has there, in your opinion, been any sign that their activities have been constrained by their relationship with the people who fund them?

Comment

Use the web resources at the end of the chapter as a way of addressing this question. You will need to access the annual reports and mission statements of the organisations. It may also be helpful to email the organisations you choose to research to ask them if they feel their activities are in any way constrained by their funders.

Social enterprise – the way forward?

It has been suggested that one way of resolving the dilemmas outlined above is to embrace these apparently contradictory pressures and utilise the methods of business and enterprise in creating new, more dynamic forms of practice. These would be able to tap into available community resources, material, intellectual, social and cultural capital to create a vision which regenerated marginalised communities and used any surpluses generated to promote local activity. This model, known as social enterprise, first rose to prominence in the UK in Bromley by Bow through the creation of a community project which was driven by the energy of a small group of activists and which sought to create, through a mixture of trading and social activity, surpluses which could be used to benefit the local area. With its classic attempt to find a third way between the state and the market it was a model embraced by New Labour, particularly as it allowed the government to claim that local self-activity could generate profit and thus reduce the burden on the state.

What then are social enterprises? It has been suggested that *there is no universally accepted definition of social enterprise, their key distinguishing features are their social aims and social ownership, combined with trading viability* (CEEDR, 2001, p4).

However, Spear suggests that social enterprises have four main characteristics in that they:

- *engage continuously in activity aimed at producing goods and/or selling services;*
- *have a high degree of autonomy – they are governed voluntarily by a group of people without control by an outside agency;*
- *engender a significant degree of economic risk – they are dependent on their members to generate sufficient income to survive;*
- *they combine voluntary and paid members but with a minimum amount of paid work.*

(Spear, 2006, p3)

The *National Strategy for Neighbourhood Renewal* report on enterprise and social exclusion (Policy Action Teams, 1999) suggested that social enterprises were important because they could play a key part in tackling social exclusion. Social enterprises can build *human and social capital... [and] strengthen local communities* (p107). They identified one of the main problems facing social enterprises as sustainability, inasmuch as there needed to be embedded support mechanisms so that they could draw down finance from various sectors of government, including 'loans' from relevant government agencies. The report notes that they differ from private-sector businesses in that *they are geared towards social regeneration and help, rather than simply the generation of profits. As such they do not fall within the standard definitions of private or public sector enterprises* (p105).

A core element of the more innovative social enterprise models is the idea of the social entrepreneur, which has been defined as *people who realise where there is an opportunity to satisfy some unmet need, and who gather together the necessary resources (generally people, often volunteers, money and premises) and use them to 'make a difference'* (Thompson, Alvy and Lees, 2000, p328). Thompson *et al.* further point out that there is nothing new in the concept of social entrepreneurship: *it was the bedrock of Victorian private hospitals, it is a key feature of charity work; it is clearly evident in the more recent hospice movement* (p328).

How then can social enterprises contribute to social work's agenda? This may happen in a number of ways. First, they tap into a core belief within social and community work that we should support people to take action to empower themselves and their communities. They appear to provide a third way between the state and private welfare which can allow people to engage with processes of change, take risks, and achieve levels of self-development. To this extent they provide a challenge to the more moribund and procedural focus still found in too much contemporary social work. Second, they relate to the changing structure of welfare in that they are a clear expression that the mixed economy of welfare does not necessarily mean an increase in managerialism or central control but that they can provide a way of allowing local people and communities to generate their own solutions to their problems. Third, the focus on the entrepreneur can at least mirror some of the ideas in the more radical alternatives which postulate the way in which community leaders can emerge organically from the local community (Freire, 1972; Gramsci, 1972).

However, these challenges to current practice need to be contextualised. The creation of social enterprises is clearly a part of the government's agenda, which while espousing the importance of the voluntary and community sectors, is doing so in a situation which seeks to unburden the state from the high levels of social expenditure with which it is currently grappling. Equally it can be seen as an attempt to 'socialise' the market so that as social workers we become even more used to competing for scarce resources against other providers. The discussion then moves from the broader radical agenda we outlined in earlier chapters, in which issues of redistribution, equity and fairness re-enter the social work vocabulary, to arguments over the distribution of diminishing resources within an increasingly inegalitarian society (Joseph Rowntree Foundation, 2006).

A more radical interpretation of social enterprise is provided through the experience of mental health service users in Trieste, Italy. Here the community has developed a service in which:

- *The human and material resources of the hospital are used to benefit the community*
- *Resources are delivered directly to the consumers*
- *Collaboration with other providers is promoted*
- *. . . [are created] productive, integrated cooperative societies that combine diversified job opportunities and vocational training with user involvement in the economical and decision making structure of the various enterprises thereby bridging the gap between the labour market and the welfare system, and providing an alternative to the inefficiency, ineffectiveness and unproductivity of welfare services.*

(Rotelli et al., n.d., pp1–2)

These discussions parallel concerns within social work about the most effective way of involving users of services and carers in decisions about service development and service delivery. We will address them in Chapter 5 before drawing out the lessons for the future directions of social work in the final chapter.

However, before leaving this discussion about the UK voluntary sector and work in the community it is worth noting the way the community development approach has been recognised across Europe. In March 2004 an international conference brought together policymakers, community workers, civil society organisations and community groups to look at how community development could contribute to the development of civil society. They agreed a common statement on community development in Europe which was known as the Budapest Declaration. They defined community development as:

A way of strengthening civil society by prioritizing the actions of communities, and their perspective in the development of social, economic and environmental policy.

(Craig, Gorman and Vereseg, 2004, pp423–9)

The declaration called for all national governments to appoint a minister with responsibility for community development and linked community development to policies around rural communities, urban regeneration, sustainability, lifelong learning and cultural development, local economic development and tackling racism and discrimination against minorities. Contributing to the debate at the conference, Hautekeur (2004) argued that *community development has most certainly found its place in the European welfare scene and in many European countries it is obtaining a higher profile* (p397).

The recent upgrading of communities to become a ministerial responsibility by the Labour government suggests that this message has been heard in the UK. However, the challenge will be to ensure that while contributing to a revitalised welfare agenda community development and community work more generally are not emasculated. As Powell (2001) has noted:

> *Support in the West for the expansion of voluntary organisations was distinctive because of its top-down character and its association with the scaling down of the welfare state. Neo-conservatives were at the forefront of this process.*

(Powell, 2001, p119)

To achieve its goals, particularly as a form of social work intervention which contributes to the empowerment of the communities, families and individuals with whom we engage community work needs to retain a radical and campaigning aspect. One of the key ways in which this can occur is through a refocusing of the attention of social and community workers to new forms of participatory practice such as those developed by the service user and carer movement. Chapter 5 looks at the potential of such approaches and at how we can ensure that any such initiatives are not merely tokenistic.

CASE STUDY

Motiv8 South Portsmouth – an enterprising voluntary organisation?

An example of a voluntary-sector organisation which seeks to engage with and empower the people with whom it works is Motiv8, a major voluntary organisation in Portsmouth which seeks to provide community alternatives for young people who have become marginalised from local services. It sees its primary role as promoting community safety through the development of services which encourage the participation and involvement of young people. The Strategic Plan for Motiv8 for 2003–6 describes the organisation's aim as being to reduce, prevent or divert young people from offending behaviour.

MOTIV8 achieves this by engaging with those most at risk of offending or those already offending.

> *Young people participate in one or more activities and receive support to increase their chances of non-offending behaviour. It works with young people aged between 8 and 25 years and the current focus is on 11–17 year olds.*

CASE STUDY *continued*

Diversion from offending can mean PREVENTING high risk young people from ever becoming involved; REDUCING young people's offending behaviour or STOPPING their offending altogether.

Motiv8 adopts a number of key approaches in its work including:

*   *youth inclusion – primary aim to promote involvement of young people through consultation, conference presentations, working with local agencies. In 2003 over half respondents to a feedback survey said that M8 had helped them in making decisions about their future, 70% rated the quality of help they received to be very good or excellent. One young person said, 'I think it has helped me to be more confident, stay out of trouble and understand more things.'*

*   *Appropriate Adult service – providing support to young people who need independent advice and assistance when arrested.*

*   *Volunteer Recruitment - offers initial training through Foundation for Youth work programme, at any one time has between 30 and 40 volunteers. One young person says, 'they helped me a lot through bad times and some behaviour problems'.*

(Motiv8 Strategic Plan 2003–6)

This activity suggests a clear focus on the delivery of accessible and accountable services to young people. The strategy makes a point of referring to continuing service development. However, at the same time the organisation needs to fit within the policy framework outlined above, particularly the focus on financial control, quality systems and on business models of service delivery. This is reflected in other sections of the strategic plan which refer to:

*   *developing active partnerships with 60 per cent of key statutory agencies;*

*   *contract compliance, successful target setting;*

*   *developing appropriate marketing strategy;*

*   *generating positive quality through annual evaluation;*

*   *passing assessment under a 'business excellence model'.*

The tension between the desire to facilitate the empowerment of the young people with whom they work and the contingencies of their funders is clearly highlighted.

An individual case study

The Youth Offending Team first referred Steven to MOTIV8 four years ago because of his offending behaviour. Since being involved with MOTIV8 he has completed his Duke of Edinburgh Bronze and Silver Awards and this year should complete his Gold Award. He was identified as being at high risk of offending and so is able to access our YIP services in Portsea. To help with his development he was a Junior Leader on MOTIV8's summer Splash holiday scheme, and has now found a job with help from our PAYP worker with 'OZ Telephones'. Once he has achieved his Gold Award he wants to return and be a volunteer to support Challenge and Adventure with other young people.

CASE STUDY *continued*

Note: Motiv8 is currently working in partnership with the local authority and the University of Portsmouth to develop a pedagogic project around the emotional well-being of young people. The approach being piloted is consistent with the discussion of pedagogy in Chapters 6 and 7.

C H A P T E R   S U M M A R Y

This chapter has sought to place the discussions in Chapters 2 and 3 in the wider social policy context. It began by reviewing developments in the UK welfare state and focused particularly on debates around the underclass, communitarianism and social exclusion. It then looked at developments in the voluntary or independent sector and examined the contradictory pressures faced by voluntary and independent sector organisations – increased funding and responsibility for the delivery of a wide range of services coupled with an increased level of accountability and control by the state. The chapter asked if this diminished the sector's capacity to engage with the more radical interventions suggested in Chapters 2 and 4.

It then looked at an area which is receiving increasing support from the government: the promotion of social enterprises and social entrepreneurship. It questioned whether this emphasis masked a commitment to less radical forms of practice as the sector grappled with the need to be financially self-reliant and to reduce dependency on the state. It looked briefly at the experience of social enterprises in Trieste as a possible alternative approach which was more consistent with a social change agenda.

FURTHER READING

Centre for Enterprise and Economic Development Research (2001) *Final report to the Small Business Service*. London: Middlesex University Business School.
A useful account of the development of social enterprises.

Jordan, B (1996) *A Theory of poverty and social exclusion.* Cambridge: Polity Press.
A stimulating and thoughtful account of the way that poverty limits the life chances of a large number of the people that social workers and community workers come into contact with. It is particularly useful in providing a counterbalance to the idea that people in poverty are passive and uninterested in changing their situation.

Jordan, B (2006) *Social policy for the twenty-first century*. Cambridge: Polity Press.
An up-to-date account of the way contemporary social work in the UK is developing, which builds on his earlier work.

Policy Action Team 3 (1999) *National strategy for neighbourhood renewal, enterprise and social exclusion.* London: HM Treasury.
One of a series of reports from the Social Exclusion Unit within the Cabinet Office. It looks specifically at the ways in which social enterprise can be used to regenerate local communities.

WEBSITES

www.Motiv8south.org.uk

www.triestesalutementale.it/inglese/allegati/Rehab.pdf

www.emes.net/fileadmin/emes/PDF_files/ELEXIES

Chapter 5

Involving, integrating or ignoring? Service users, carers and social work

This chapter will help you begin to meet the following National Occupational Standards for social work.

Key Role 1: Prepare for and work with individuals, families, carers, groups and communities to assess their needs and circumstances.
- Work with individuals, families, carers, groups and communities to enable them to analyse, identify, clarify and express their strengths, expectations and limitations.
- Work with individuals, families, carers, groups and communities to enable them to assess and make informed decisions about their needs, circumstances, risks, preferred options and resources.

Key Role 2: Plan, carry out, review and evaluate social work practice, with individuals, families, carers, groups, communities and other professionals.
- Develop and maintain relationships with individuals, families, carers, groups, communities and others.
- Help groups to achieve planned outcomes for their members and to evaluate the appropriateness of their work.

Key Role 3: Support individuals to represent their needs, views and circumstances.
- Advocate for, and with individuals, families, carers, groups and communities.
- Work with individuals, families, carers, groups and communities to select the best form of representation for decision-making forums.
- Enable individuals, families, carers, groups and communities to be involved in decision-making forums.

Key Role 4: Manage risk to individuals, families, carers, groups and communities.
- Balance the rights and responsibilities of individuals, families, carers, groups and communities with associated risk.

Key Role 5: Manage and be accountable, with supervision and support for your own social work practice within your organisation.
- Carry out duties using accountable professional judgement and knowledge-based social work practice.
- Contribute to monitoring the quality of the services provided.
- Share records with individuals, families, carers, groups and communities.
- Deal constructively with disagreements and conflict within relationships.

Key Role 6: Demonstrate professional competence in social work practice.
- Work within the principles and values underpinning social work practice.
- Devise strategies to deal with ethical issues, dilemmas and conflicts.
- Contribute to policy review and development.

QAA Benchmarking Statement

1.12 The term 'service user' is used in this statement to cover the wide and diverse set of individuals, groups and organisations who are involved in, or who benefit from, the contribution of social work to the well being of society. ...In providing services, social workers should engage with service users in ways that are characterised by openness, reciprocity, mutual accountability and explicit recognition of the powers of the social worker and the legal context of intervention.

National Occupational Standards for Community Work

Key Role A: *Develop working relationships with communities and organisations.*

Key Role B1: *Contribute to the development of community groups/networks.*

B2: *Facilitate the development of community groups and networks.*

B3: *Facilitate ways of working collaboratively.*

Key Role C1: *Work within communities to select options and make plans for collective action.*

C2: *Contribute to collective action within a community.*

C3: *Support communities to plan and take collective action.*

C4: *Ensure community participation in planning and taking collective action.*

C6: *Work with communities to identify needs, opportunities, rights and responsibilities.*

Key Role D1: *Support communities to monitor and review action for change.*

D2: *Facilitate the development of evaluation networks.*

Key Role E4: *Develop people's skills and roles within community groups/networks.*

E5: *Facilitate the development of people and learning in communities.*

E6: *Develop and review community based organisational structures.*

E7: *Develop and maintain organisational frameworks for community based initiatives.*

Introduction

The last three chapters have illustrated how social and community work are dynamic activities which possess traditions that can be drawn on to inform current practice. Radical activity now needs to be reframed so that the potential illustrated in Chapters 2 and 3 can be articulated within the changing welfare mix which we described in Chapter 4. How can we connect these apparently divergent analyses? The concept of inclusion can enable us to see how these historical and contemporary analyses converge. A fully developed concept of inclusion also enables us to locate power as a central part of any analysis of social and community work's potential for change. It particularly helps us to see people who use social work services as active agents in changing their own situation and challenging the perspective of agencies with whom they work.

An insight into the importance of engaging with the people who use services is provided in the writings of Michel Foucault. When asked why he looked at the local rather than structural aspect of political problems, Foucault said:

> *the problems which I try to address . . . which involve daily life, cannot be easily resolved. It takes many years, decades of work carried out at grass roots level with the people directly involved, and the right to speech and political imagination must be returned to them . . . the complexity of the problem will be able to appear in its connection with people's lives . . . the object is to proceed a little at a time, to introduce modifications that are capable of, if not finding a solution, then at least changing the givens of a problem.*
>
> (Foucault, 1981, pp158–9)

While Foucault was addressing issues of political power in the broad sense, his comments can just as easily be seen as a prime legitimation for social workers' concern with involving service users. Work with service users is specifically about releasing people's political imagination so that they can envision an alternative experience, a different way of experiencing and delivering welfare and social work services. It is also about focusing on the particular daily experience of those people most directly involved in services – service users. It is particularly concerned with changing the way issues are framed so that service users are not seen as 'problems' or 'clients' but rather as active partners in changing the services they directly experience. This approach means therefore that when examining service user involvement we need to ask whether the involvement we are discussing is real or tokenistic. Before seeking to integrate Foucault into our analysis we will first focus on: how a concern with service user involvement originated; the legislative and policy context within which it has developed; the increasing involvement of service users in the development and delivery of social work education; and the international context within which debates about service user involvement, which are essentially about the meaning of our welfare system, can be understood. We will then seek to develop a model for evaluating service user involvement which integrates Foucault and other key social and political theory.

The origins of service user involvement

The involvement of service users in service delivery and development is now so firmly embedded in legislation and policy that it is easy to forget that it was not that long ago that the role of service users was seen as a much more marginal one. The idea of empowerment had been central to at least some social work discourses since the 1980s (Bandana 1985; Dominelli, 1988; Adams, 1990) and arguably since the 'radical social work' movement of the 1970s (Bailey and Brake, 1975; Corrigan and Leonard, 1978; Bailey and Brake, 1980) and can be seen as the key concept which emerged out of the radical social work movement, which:

> sought to generate a wider awareness of the power that social workers had by virtue of their access to information and sources that were not readily available to service users. 'Empowerment' was the process of transferring this power into the hands of the people who were systematically denied it within the framework of the Welfare State.
>
> (Langan and Lee, 1989, p9; see Chapter 2)

Probably the first examples of user involvement come from the users/survivors of the mental health system, which emerged from the anti-psychiatry and civil rights movements in the 1960s (MIND, 2005). However, the idea of involving service users as partners in service delivery did not really take off until the early 1990s when the Social Services Inspectorate said of the National Health Service and Community Care Act 1990, *the rationale for this development is the empowerment of service users* (quoted in Philpot, 1993, p1). Equally, the Children Act 1989 was *peppered with references to the need to inform, consult and involve people who use services* (Braye, 2000, p13). However, from the beginning the process of user involvement was often poorly articulated and confused in its implementation, As Braye (2000) notes, *the legal mandate for participation and involvement may be criticised as partial, contradictory and ineffectual* (p15).

An example of this confusion and contradiction can be seen in the development of policies around disability, particularly around community care and direct payments, both of which were supposed to empower and give a voice to people with disabilities. As Priestly argues, *the first assumption of community care policy is that disabled people are dependent and need 'care'* (Priestly, 1999, p43). Looking at the direct payments legislation, he says *the administrative and professional dominance over the assessment of 'need' remain largely unchallenged* (p202). Moreover, these discussions remain locked into discourses around the individual/medical model of disability which we examined in Chapter 2. As Oliver noted when reviewing the development of these policies, *there was little evidence that disabled people were being involved in the planning and delivery of services in the way that legislation had required* (Oliver, 2003, p314).

Largely this was because professionals and legislators failed to appreciate the capacity of people with disabilities to make their own choices about the type and quality of service they wished to access. As Hersov (1992) suggested:

> *the first obstacle towards* believing *that people with learning difficulties can begin to make real choices and decisions in their lives is our own reluctance to acknowledge the possibility that they might be able to do so. This may be a legacy of viewing this group of people as eternal children who will always need their parents (or other carers) to help them function and cope: it may also reflect our own discomfort when they demonstrate that they don't need us anymore.*

(Hersov, 1992, p286)

The lesson, he suggests, is that people with disabilities should be given choices over decisions which affect their lives as illustrated by the following case study.

CASE STUDY

Women First

An interesting account of the ways in which women with learning disabilities sought to develop their own methods of self organisation is provided by Jan Walmsley (1993). She described the Women First Conference, a national conference for women with learning disabilities. She pointed out that the planning and the running of the conference was an exercise in involving women with learning difficulties in a national event which addressed their interest *(p87). She demonstrates the ways in which professionals and carers were not allowed to outnumber women with learning disabilities within the conference. She points out also how although women obviously attended the conference on the basis of a common recognition of their experiences of learning difficulties, it became quite clear that within even the group of women who attended the conference there was a wide diversity in experience and expectation. Discussions in groups emerged around abuse, race, sexuality and HIV/Aids.*

CASE STUDY *continued*

Walmsley argues:

> *Women First was an important event, a milestone in delineating the right of women with learning difficulties to have their interests aired, discussed, recorded and written about. As an exercise in participation, it deserves recognition, and has some valuable messages for others embarking on a similar enterprise.*
>
> *(p97)*

She pointed to lessons that can be learned from such a conference, particularly about ensuring the real and not tokenistic involvement of people with learning disabilities in such an event.

During the mid-1990s there was little sign that policymakers or legislators were acknowledging the importance of people with learning disabilities exerting greater control over their lives. Ramscharan *et al.* (1997, p256) argued that people with learning disabilities should have *sufficient entitlement to resources to prevent oppression and inequality, and maximise self-determination and participation...such participation and inclusion...provide the conditions under which citizens with learning disabilities make choices about their everyday lives*. It was 2001 before this began to become central to social policy (see discussion of *Valuing people* in Section 5.4 and Chapter 1).

Legislative and policy context

Over the last few years this situation has changed. Service users have at last been recognised as having a significant role in the delivery, management and development of welfare services. This is reflected in the attention given to service user involvement in both the legislative and policy contexts. These debates cut across all service boundaries and raise questions about service user representation (Beresford and Campbell, 1994), the efficacy of current initiatives (SCIE, 2004) and the usefulness of the service user perspective across a range of service user areas: young people (Freeman *et al.*, 1996; Hayden *et al.*, 1999; Children's Rights Alliance and National Youth Council of Ireland, 2003); people in poverty (Bennett and Roberts, 2004; Beresford and Hoban, 2005); evaluating community outcomes (Cassidy and Jakes, undated) parents (Gustafson and Driver, 2005); homeless people (Phillips, 2004); and with traditional service user groups such as people with mental health problems, people with disabilities and older people.

The drivers behind these initiatives have often been service users themselves. The role of disability activists in creating the political climate to support anti-discriminatory legislation around disability is well known (Beresford and Campbell, 1994; Campbell and Oliver, 1996; Hughes, 1998), as is their role in ensuring that the Disability Discrimination Act 1995 was amended to give disabled people the right to enforcement action if their entitlements were not met. Equally, the voice of the service user can be seen in the *Valuing people* White Paper and subsequent policy developments which grew out of that. The White Paper enshrined the concepts of rights, independence, choice, inclusion, and argued that *people with learning disabilities have little control over their lives... The Government's objective is to enable people with learning disabilities to have as much choice and control as possible over their lives and the services and support they receive* (Department of Health, 2001, p4). It recognised the capacity of people with learning disabilities to take control of their lives and suggested that people should be supported to become self-advocates because:

> The growth of the self-advocacy movement shows how people with learning disabilities can make a real difference to service development and delivery. Citizen advocates make a vital contribution to enabling the voices of people with more complex disabilities to be heard.
>
> (p46)

Service user involvement has also been built into other policy initiatives. The Green Paper on adult social care, *Independence, well-being and choice* argued that *we want to move to a system where adults are able to take greater control of their lives* (DoH, 2005a, p10). The Green Paper further emphasises this point when it says *we want to give people greater choice and control over how their needs shall be met* (p11). Following the Green Paper the Social Care Institute of Excellence (SCIE) published a report by Wistow, which was based on initial consultations around England with service users. This part of the research, conducted by Shaping Our Lives, an independent user-controlled organisation, reported that service users had *strong, well thought-out ideas* about the future of social care (Wistow, 2005, p3). The responses to the consultation supported these earlier conclusions and emphasised that part of this greater choice and control should be *the desire expressed by many people who use services to have more control over the risks they would choose to take to lead more independent lives* (DoH, 2005b, p6). The management of risk was an important element in the responses received. As the paper says:

> Many powerful comments were made about how the approach to managing risk affects people's lives, the choices they make and the independence and well-being they experience.
>
> (DoH, 2005b, p19)

This mirrors a central concern of current social policy of which it has been said key elements are *issues of blame, defensibility and rationing. The social work of the personal social services is no longer about collectivist provision to those sections of society deemed to be 'in need', it is a residual service for those both at risk and posing a risk* (Kemshall, 2002, p89). In this context we are dealing with a system which seeks to manage risk for reasons of professional control and resource restraint and there must therefore be concern about how far social work agencies will go in promoting risk when it may result in the generation of extra demands on resources.

Hudson, Dearey and Glendenning (2004) produced a scoping report which attempts to establish the views of service users about adult social care. They highlight the concern among service users to *be in control and make their own decisions about their lives. Ensuring independence... is arguably the most important outcome for adult social care service users* (p6). From their reading of the literature they identified ten service principles that service delivery should be based upon. These included a personalised service model, a choice and diversity model and a user empowerment model. They suggested that the latter should be based on a social model of ageing and disability, which places the emphasis on rights as well as needs. This focus on rights would, they argued, *transform the nature of current debate and social care practice* (p13). User empowerment could be further facilitated by the development of user-controlled services, similar to the model in Centres for Independent Living, and by *the promotion of collective user 'voices' and of effective service responses to those voices* (p13).

The Welsh Assembly Government produced policy implementation guidance for Adult Mental Health Services in 2004. Their report, *Stronger in partnership*, sought to develop guidance as to the best way of involving people who use mental health services in the design, planning, delivery and evaluation of those services. They argued that genuine service user involvement requires:

- building confidence;
- providing relevant and timely information;
- providing suitable space and time;
- responding appropriately.

This involved recognising service users as experts in their experience, allowing service users to bring their own perspectives about treatment and care in a way that can lead service providers to re-evaluate their services and as a way of *enabling people to feel that they are being listened to and that their contribution is being valued. Working collectively as part of a network of groups can help people increase their confidence and raise self-esteem* (Welsh Assembly Government, 2004, pp8–9).

Similar developments can be seen in children's services. The recent report from the Commission for Social Care Inspection (CSCI), *Making every child matter*, recognised the importance of listening to young people in the public care system if we are to get a clear view of the way children's services are developing and of whether they were meeting the needs of young people. They comment in the report that:

> *Looked after children and young people appear to be increasingly positive about their experiences. Many tell us they are generally treated well, their views sought and their rights explained and that their lives have improved since they became involved with children's services.*
>
> (CSCI, 2005, p6)

This picture is not, however, always reflected at local level and members of Care Can Change, a group of young people with experience of the care system in the South East, have expressed a more measured and critical attitude towards their experience (Bown, 2005).

Organisations working with the homeless are also exploring issues around service user involvement with a service user group which is probably more unpredictable and chaotic than most. Shelter support the CHiP network (Changing Homelessness in Practice), which has produced a guide to service user involvement in homelessness. They note, *the 'trouble' with service user involvement is that it is a remarkably simple concept, but its apparent simplicity is also a key to its complexity* (Shelter, 2004, p2).

They suggest that there are three priorities if we want to make service user involvement work:

- *the development of statements and policies to reflect a commitment to service user involvement;*
- *practical support to engage service users;*
- *genuine engagement at a strategic planning level.*

As they note, *it is counter productive to develop the capacity of people affected by homelessness and the organizations and workers who support them, but invest no time, energy or money in ensuring that key decision making bodies are receptive and involved in the process* (Shelter, 2004, pp6–7).

The way such debates are now reflected across the welfare spectrum is further illustrated in *Improving services, improving lives*, an interim report from the Social Exclusion Unit within the Office of the Deputy Prime Minister. The report looked at what changes needed to be made in the delivery of public services to meet the needs of disadvantaged people. One of the six key themes identified within the report was the need to build personal capacity. The authors argued that this was important because:

> *People are more likely to get what they need from services if they are equipped with confidence and self-esteem, communication skills that enable them to articulate their needs, and knowledge of how the system works. These kinds of capacity have a key role to play in helping to build aspirations and ensuring that people benefit from mechanisms for involving users in public service delivery.*
>
> (ODPM, 2005, p7)

This quote illustrates the extent to which the rhetoric of empowerment has now become part of the general welfare discourse in the UK.

ACTIVITY 5.1

What are the key issues identified by the researchers/organisations looking into service user involvement? How do these link to the discussion of empowerment and advocacy in earlier chapters?

Comment

You will need to refer back to discussions in earlier chapters. At this stage it is helpful to focus on the issue of risk and the way in which people who use services and service providers conceptualise risk quite differently.

Service users in social work education

Not surprisingly, given this wide-scale endorsement of the principle of service user/carer inclusion and participation, there has been a significant increase in the level of service user involvement in social work education. As a contributor to the Living and Learning Together Conference said:

> *We are determined to teach social work students because we do not want anybody to go through what we went through and we want services to be better.*
>
> (Workshop contributor. Living and Learning Together Conference, SCIE, 2004a, p36)

This quote illustrates the importance service users attribute to their having a greater role in training and educating social workers. Their concern is not just to highlight issues but to contribute to the development and improvement of services. The decision by the General Social Care Council to provide financial support for service user involvement in social work education in the new degree, from 2003, provided a welcome impetus to service user involvement in social work education. Such an involvement is essential if services are to be able to meet the demands placed on them in the new welfare mix. SCIE (2004b) have noted the connection between values underpinning service user organisations and social work. They argue:

> *The service user movement emphasises the importance of models of participation that are based on human rights, equalities, inclusion and the social model of disability. Their approaches seek to empower people and counter oppressive and discriminatory practice. There is overlap between the values of service user-controlled organisations and those of social work and social care.*
>
> (SCIE, 2004, p11)

SCIE (2004b) suggest that service users should be involved at a strategic and management level with universities. This may include involvement at programme management and partnership levels (although this is an area of collaboration and partnership which remains underdeveloped at present). It is more likely to focus on:

- selecting students;
- teaching and learning provision;
- placement learning opportunities – the opportunity to work with and within service user-controlled organisations (the recently formed Learning Resource Centre Networks are in some cases funding work to develop such placements and to support service user-controlled organisations to offer placements);
- assessment of students;
- quality assurance.

Peter Beresford argues that to achieve such a level of involvement will entail a focus on values – treating service users with honesty, openness, respect, equality and of course commitment, and strategy, which will involve *a fundamental culture change. We will all need to do things differently and changes in practice – supporting service user training, developing user-controlled organisations, addressing diversity, research, evaluation and payment* (SCIE, 2004b, pp12–14). The issue of payment is a major one, particularly if we are to demonstrate to service users that we value their involvement at a real rather than tokenistic level. As Levin noted, *prompt and acceptable payment arrangements are key to the success of recruiting service user and carer trainers and retaining them* (Levin, 2004, p28). Unfortunately this remains an issue particularly for those service users and carers claiming benefits despite the recent report from SCIE (Turner and Beresford, 2005).

Wilson and Beresford (2000) have warned against a simplistic attempt to suggest that a commitment to anti-oppressive values of itself ensures that service users views are heard and respected. Instead they argue that:

> *Such a theory [of anti-oppressive practice] is by definition reliant upon user knowledge and ideas. Social work's adoption of a façade of 'anti-oppressive practice' which in reality appropriates and incorporates the knowledge and experiences of service users, whilst retaining the power to determine just what it is that counts as 'anti-oppressive' is for us the most oppressive aspect of its anti-oppressive stance.*
>
> (Wilson and Beresford, 2000, p565)

They conclude that anti-oppressive practice needs to be re-evaluated to ensure that it properly reflects service users' views and aspirations. One way of ensuring this in the academic environment is to recognise that service user involvement should be across the curriculum and not just in those areas where the service users are deemed to be experts because of their experience of a particular service. Davis and Wainwright (2005) provide a useful reminder that even within the protected environs of academia a focus on social work's potential to change the life chances of the poorest sections of society should not be forgotten. ATD Fourth World have recently pointed to the importance, following the Laming Report and *Every child matters*, of services developing an *increased understanding of family poverty across professional disciplines* (ATD Fourth World, 2005, p8). They report on a joint project between the Family Rights Group, ATD Fourth World and Royal Holloway, University of London, which aimed to:

- *bring together the experience of people living in poverty (who are service users) and the experience of academics and social work practitioners;*
- *build an understanding between families living in poverty and those responsible for training social workers;*
- *develop a pilot training project.*

They concluded that *the project has demonstrated the importance of involving service users in respect of designing (as well as participating) in its work programme* (p28). This is an important reminder of how service user involvement needs to be mainstreamed rather than regarded as an add-on, even if that is value added, of social work education.

In response to this growing demand for greater service user/carer involvement in social work education, the Care Council for Wales has produced a set of standards for involving Service users and carers in the social work degree in Wales (Care Council for Wales, 2005). These are set out in Table 5.1.

Table 5.1 Standards for involving Service Users and Carers in the degree in Wales

Five Standards about developing and sustaining involvement

- Finding the people who might want to be involved.
- Agreeing principles for working together.
- Incorporating a strategy and plan for service user and carer involvement into the overall plan for the degree.
- Agreements for support arrangements and facilities.
- Contracts and protocols.

Four standards about the range of involvement

- In strategic planning and management of the programme.
- In recruitment and selection.
- In teaching and practice learning.
- In assessment.

One standard on quality assurance

Source: Care Council for Wales, 2005, pp11–28

The Care Council for Wales outlines ten standards to sustain and develop service user and carer involvement in the new degree; the level of involvement which this entails and the service user/carer role in quality assurance.

A practical example, of what this can mean to a social work programme is provided by the Service User Inclusion Group (SUIG) at the University of Portsmouth.

CASE STUDY

Service User Inclusion Group (SUIG), University of Portsmouth

SUIG was formed in June 2004 with support of money provided by the General Social Care Council to secure the involvement of service users in the delivery of social work education. Since its formation the group has been involved in:

- *interviewing and admissions procedures;*
- *teaching – the group was one of the pilot groups chosen by Skills for Care to deliver a training programme to train service users to teach on the Portsmouth social work degree programme;*
- *assessing students 'Fitness for Practice' at the end of Level One;*
- *assessing student presentations;*
- *assessing presentations by applicants seeking academic positions;*
- *redesigning the curricula;*
- *auditing work placements – the group is currently designing an audit tool to assess whether placement agencies meet students' learning needs;*
- *producing a video, 'What I want from a social worker';*

- *developing a range of drama and cultural activities for use in social work training;*
- *small-scale research around homelessness.*

SUIG has not yet been involved in course management, partly because of university fears about undermining academic judgement. However, this remains a goal and will arguably be the test of where the Group sits within the involvement framework discussed below.

SUIG's experience can help illustrate the point made by Foucault at the beginning of this chapter about the pace at which we are seeking to secure meaningful change. He speaks of the need to proceed a little at a time. Yet many agencies, in the desire to be seen to be ticking all the right boxes, treat service user involvement as if it is an immediate imperative and the service user should sublimate their own needs to achieve it. In 2005 SUIG, along with a number of other service user organisations, were commissioned, by TOPSS (the Training Organisation for the Personal Social Services; now Skills for Care) to undertake training of service users to enable them to teach on the new social work degree. After successfully tendering for the contract, SUIG was encouraged to pilot a training programme in two cities in the South. This involved recruiting service users for the programmes and supposedly would include piloting training material developed by TOPSS. When the agreed start date for the training arrived, TOPSS had not produced the relevant training material and the group needed to develop their own. TOPSS appeared to think that training could be easily rescheduled. They had no conception that service users were themselves extremely busy people with their own schedules and they also appeared to be unaware that SUIG members had their own expectations and aspirations, which they had invested in the programme (SUIG, 2005). Eventually the hard copies of the training material arrived after the project had finished. This further illustrates the point made by Wilson and Beresford (2000) when they spoke of how there was a real danger that service users' views and aspirations could be appropriated by larger, more powerful, professional or sectoral organisations.

Consider how students and/or lecturers on social work programmes can ensure greater service user involvement? Which of those levels of involvement discussed in the above case study apply in your university/college? How can you increase the degree of service user involvement?

Comment

Look at the SCIE website and read their papers on service user involvement. Use their analysis to supplement the above discussion.

International dimensions to service user involvement

Evers (2004) has suggested that we can distinguish between five discourses around user involvement in Europe, raising an important point: service user involvement is not a particularly UK phenomena. Writing as part of the Expert Group on Service User Involvement for the Council of Europe, he argues that in Europe we can see five models of service user involvement (see also Council of Europe, 2004).

These models are welfarism, professionalism, consumerism, managerialism and participationism. *Welfarism* is characterised by a top-down approach to participation; *professionalism* can be identified as indicating that the welfare professional does things for rather than in partnership with the service user; *consumerism* is predicated on the idea of the market and the belief that the service user can be given choice and exit options through which their preferences can be gauged. *Managerialism* is an approach which puts the provider rather than the user at the centre and which focuses on managerial imperatives such as effectiveness and efficiency. The final category is *participationism,* of which Evers says *the specific point of participationism . . . is the belief that people should engage personally in the shaping of services* (Evers, 2004, p7). Participationism, he suggests, emphasises localism and diversity and can be seen to be a bottom-up approach to participation which may only have a small impact on complex mainstream services such as hospitals or the labour market. It does pose a challenge as it is based *on a very demanding concept of the user as co-producer* (p7). As such this model would appear to be much closer to the partnership approach this chapter attempts to develop and which is discussed below.

A range of service user initiatives have also been seen in other European countries (Shulze and Wirth, 1996). Heikkila and Julkunen (2003) produced a report for the Council of Europe which documented the barriers to service user involvement across Europe. Their research was one of the outcomes of the work of the Group of Specialists on User Involvement in Social Services and Integrated Service Delivery commissioned by the European Committee for Social Cohesion (CDCS). This research identified a number of key principles for service user involvement in social services which should be applied across all countries (Council of Europe, 2004, p5). These were:

- involvement as a right and responsibility – there should be a democratic right for service users to be involved;
- centrality of service user involvement in agencies' mission statements;
- access to services – the provision of services in sufficient quantity and quality;
- importance of evidence – through relevant research;
- culture of user involvement – a consistent commitment from different service sectors;
- users as recipients and actors – service users are not passive recipients but should play a full role in social care;
- taking account of users' networks – the need to recognise the key people involved with service users to maximise their involvement.

As part of this research Heikkila and Julkunen (2003) identified a number of examples of good practice, which are outlined in Table 5.2.

Table 5.2 Examples of good practice across Europe

Country	General comment	Practice exemplar	Outcomes
Netherlands	'a culture of client and user participation' (p7)	Prevention and combating of Poverty and Social Exclusion Act 1997	Created statutory right to client participation
Denmark	Welfare state moved from central planning to decentralisation	Bikva-model – based on idea that concept of quality is problematised and evaluated from user perspective	At end 1990s Ministry of Social Affairs established project to make service users more active in quality development
Norway	Pioneer of voluntary centres – integrated cooperation between municipalities and voluntary organisations	Fattighuset – a client organisation addressing political issues around poverty	'a good example of a country which has exceptionally active client organisation that addresses poverty issues' (p7)
Sweden	Country with strong legislative structures for user involvement	Long tradition of advocates, 'gode man' representing people in vulnerable groups	Social Services Act is 'considered to be based on an empowerment model'; 'services should be delivered so as they empower users' (p8)

Source: adapted from Heikkila and Julkunen 2003, p7, downloaded from www.coe.int/T/E/Social_cohesion/social_Policies/04.Activities/1.Access_to-soc

The analysis of Heikkila and Julkunen (2003) demonstrates that the UK is not alone in seeing involvement and inclusion as key elements of social work practice. They draw attention to the way in which the Scandinavian countries have a particular commitment to working with service users. Sweden enshrines the approach in a clear legislative structure and Norway has a strong tradition of partnership between municipalities (local authorities) and voluntary organisations which underpins their commitment to service user involvement.

ACTIVITY 5.3

Using the above analysis, think about the organisation you are currently working in (or in which you are undertaking your practice or work placement). Plot along the matrix how you see your organisation scores in respect of these issues.

Indicator of good practice	Very Good Score 5	Good Score 4	Satis- factory Score 3	Poor Score 2	Very Poor Score 1
SUs have right to involvement					
Included in Mission Statement					
Service users' needs met					
Consistent commitment to involvement across organisation					
SUs actively involved					
Relates to SU network					

Key: Maximum level of Service User Involvement 30, minimum 6

Task: How can you change your organisation's score?

- *How does your organisation score on the above matrix?*
- *What factors account for that score?*
- *How could the score be increased, or maximised*

Heikkila and Julkunen (2003) identified a number of barriers to effective service user involvement. These are shown in Table 5.3.

Table 5.3 Barriers to good practice

Potential barriers	Cause
Political/legal obstacles	Lack of clear legislative rights, existence of some legislation which mitigates against involvement
Administrative barriers	Lack of clear goals and knowledge of good practice
Professional barriers	Social workers not used to ceding control, 'activation of service users can be seen and felt as an extra burden for hard working professionals' (p9)
Language barriers	Both in sense of service users and social workers speaking different languages but also in sense of them coming from different viewpoints
Personal barriers	Different attitudes and views on involvement – service users' focus may be financial independence and decent living conditions, social workers may focus on self-activity and self-reliance

Source: adapted from Heikkila and Julkunen, 2003, p9, downloaded from www.coe.int/T/E/Social_cohesion/social_Policies/04.Activities/1.Access_to-soc

The barriers they identify relate to issues of professional power and accountability as well as those of organisational culture and tradition. Getting professionals to cede power to people who use services is extremely difficult and cuts across the trends towards creating professional expertise and knowledge which current developments in social work in the UK are beginning to embrace. These issues will be dealt with in greater detail in the next chapter.

ACTIVITY 5.4

Using the following matrix, evaluate how your organisation can overcome the barriers to good practice identified in this research.

Potential barriers	Cause	Solution
Political/legal obstacles		
Administrative barriers		
Professional barriers		
Language barriers		
Personal barriers		

Applying this analysis to your organisation (or practice or work placement), how would these factors improve the way it related to service users?

Comment

It is worth looking in detail at the articles by Heikkila and Julkunen and by Evers. Also look at the SCIE website.

Heikkila and Julkunen (2003) concluded that better involvement could be achieved by:

- *Greater service user and NGO involvement in social services*
- *The development of effective strategies for service user involvement including financial support and the development of user boards*
- *Learning systematically form current experience*
- *Putting in place proper support frameworks*
- *Use of a variety of approaches.*

(Heikkila and Julkunen, 2003, pp9–10)

Reflections from the UK

Examples of how improved service user involvement can be achieved can be found in the UK. Service users at the Making Service User Involvement Effective seminar, held at the University of Portsmouth in 2003, made similar points. This seminar was specifically designed to promote the role of service users within social work (University of Portsmouth, 2003). The focus on the presentations by the Citizens as Trainers Group (CAT) from Salford and the Service User Forum in Portsmouth was on how such involvement can move beyond tokenism to ensure that the voice of service users is really heard in service practice and development. As the CAT group said in their presentation:

> *User-consultation can be slow and not fit into bureaucratic deadlines but it's central to good social care . . . we are your equals and you are asking our advice . . . start off with a blank sheet, not something you have already compiled and you just want us to say 'OK' to. That's not consultation, it's tokenism. Let us be there from the start, alongside you.*

The Service User Forum reminded the audience that the National Service Framework for Mental Health Services had said *service users need to be involved in planning and delivery of care* and that they were there to *help give a voice in helping to shape mental health services within Portsmouth City now and in the future.*

As the report of the seminar says:

> *To start with we can begin valuing the contribution service users can make to service development and improvement. We need to move beyond an approach, which uses the involvement of one or two service users to validate decisions already made about the way social work services are run. We also need to recognize that service user involvement is a powerful tool, which can equip service users to overcome their own sense of powerlessness.*

> *When this happens it is probable that service users will place increasing demands on our services and will become even less inclined to accept poor standards of service delivery. That is the challenge for all agencies in the social work/social care field.*
>
> (University of Portsmouth, 2003, p4)

Making service user involvement effective

How then can we utilise this understanding of both the barriers to involvement and good practice around involvement to construct a model of service user participation and involvement? This presents a major challenge for social work in the changing welfare environment. How can we make service user involvement effective, real and sustainable and avoid the problems of agency inertia, organisational blockage and tokenistic response? How do we measure the effectiveness of service user involvement? How do we ensure that agencies involve service users not just as lay consultants but as real, active and equal participants in all aspects of social work?

A number of ways of evaluating service user involvement can be seen in the literature and a possible model for evaluating service user involvement can be constructed which draws on the best of these initiatives.

Developing an evaluative framework

Debates around participation and involvement are not new and can be traced back to earlier discussions around radical social work and community action (see Chapter 3). However, there has been little research into the impact of service user participation and involvement on service provision (Carr, 2004). Carr has suggested that one of *the principle barriers identified in the literature are the power differentials and dynamics between service users and professionals* (Carr, 2004, p14). Indeed she argues that:

Exclusionary structures, institutional practices and attitudes can still affect the extent to which service users can influence change. It appears that power sharing can be difficult within established mainstream structures, formal consultation mechanisms and traditional ideologies.

(p14)

How then can we evaluate the way these processes operate? Is it possible to produce an evaluation framework which can allow us to make explicit the way these processes operate? One of the earliest attempts to provide a framework for evaluating participation is provided by Sherry Arnstein, who developed her 'ladder of citizen participation' in 1969. Arnstein suggested that *there is a real difference between going through the empty ritual of participation and having the real power needed to affect the outcome of the process* (Arnstein, 1969, p215). She argued that a central concern is the redistribution of power *that enables the have-not citizens, presently excluded from the political and economic processes, to be deliberately included in the future* (p214).

Her model suggests that participation can be evaluated along a typology of eight levels of participation, which she identifies as follows (see Figure 5.1). *Therapy* and *manipulation* constitute levels of non-participation in which those with power seek to cure or educate those seeking power. *Informing* and *consulting* are characteristic where people are encouraged to articulate their views but lack the power to have them implemented. With *placation* these elements are characterised by tokenism in which *the ground rules allow the have-nots to advise, but retain for the power-holders the continued right to decide* (Arnstein, 1969, p216). The final three levels illustrate increasing levels of influence and power until at the level of *citizen control, have-not citizens obtain the majority of decision-making seats or full managerial power* (p216). This she argues is where citizen control rests.

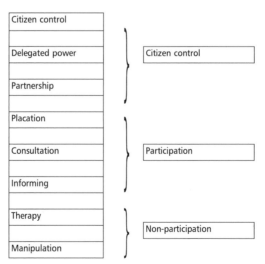

Figure 5.1 Arnstein's ladder of participation

The language used is similar to that used by other 'radical liberals' such as Alinsky, who equally couches his analysis in the rather simplistic language of 'haves' and 'have-nots' (Alinsky,1972). However, the analysis does point to the dangers of accepting at face value agencies' and institutions' claims that they are seeking to increase levels of participation, promote involvement and empowerment and work in partnership with service users. Such claims can, through this model and those discussed below, at least be subjected to analysis and argumentation.

This model has been taken on and developed by others to suggest a more complex way of mapping involvement. Burns, Hambleton and Hoggett (1994) applied the model to local authority participation strategies in London and suggested that Arnstein's ladder could be expanded to include 12 factors. Retaining the distinction between citizen control, citizen participation and citizen non-participation, they suggest that a ladder of citizen empowerment might be impacted upon by the nature of the decision-making process. On one level they see decisions being mediated by the behaviour and performance of staff (operational practices), the way money is spent (operational decisions) and by the strategic objectives of a particular service (policy-making) (p160). On another level the major factor may be what Hirschmann (1970) has called 'exit' and 'voice'. Exit is defined as the withdrawal of support for a service from those using it. Voice is where dissatisfaction is more actively articulated through protest or action (Burns, Hambleton and Hoggett, 1994, pp162–3).

ACTIVITY 5.5

- *Think about a service user involvement process you have been involved in.*
- *Where would you place that example of service user involvement on this participation ladder?*
- *What were the key factors that led you to this decision?*
- *Would you describe that process as one of exit or choice?*

Comment

You should by now be undertaking your practice placement. Use the organisation within which you are placed as the reference point for this activity.

At this stage it is worth highlighting another factor: the role people play in participation strategies. Simmons and Birchall (2005) suggest that levels of participation are affected by the type of activist who was participating. They distinguished between five types of activists:

- campaigners – very active and confident in participation, seeking change rather than the *status quo*;
- foot soldiers – quite committed but at different level, often undertook group's support functions;
- thinkers rather than doers – more likely to be educationally qualified and interested in participation as a learning experience;
- habitual participants – guided by internalised norms, part of a regular programme of involvement;
- marginal participants – less active and motivated, relatively uncommitted.

Simmons and Birchall suggested that to make participation effective it was therefore necessary to recognise that participation is an activity mediated by a variety of factors: time, resources, skills, motivation. They suggest that it is possible to construct a 'participation chain' to explain levels of participation. This may consist of a number of key factors including motivation, resources and the level at which people mobilise to become involved.

They found that income levels did not impact on involvement and that time was a resource barrier that could be surmounted. However, skills (indicated by educational qualification, previous experiences and training) appeared to be *very important for service users both in getting started and in supporting higher levels of participation* (Simmons and Birchall, 2005, p272). Mobilisation was strongly impacted upon, they suggested, by 'catalysing issues', which, in relation to public services included:

> negative relationships with authorities ('authorities are not listening to people like me', 'authorities cannot be trusted to make decisions on behalf of people like me'), a sense of relative deprivation ('my community is worse off than other similar communities') and a desire for change ('change is not happening quickly enough').
>
> (pp272–3)

Their research led them to suggest a fourth factor governing people's involvement; this was what they term the 'dynamics of participation', which they suggest is impacted upon by cultural and institutional factors.

Quoting DETR research, they argue that *people often hold a positive view of their experience of participation. This may lead to the affirmation of participants' key motivations and to the development over time of a commitment to participate* (DETR, 1998, p273). These factors are in turn impacted upon by the group of which they are a member in so far as *the group can play an important role in the transformation of individuals' motivations over time. This may involve the promotion of collectivistic motivations to a primary position in people's 'motivational hierarchy'* (p275).

Integrating theory and practice

This discussion suggests that the research evidence, theoretical frameworks and participation models which emerge can start to provide us with a way of integrating the theory and practice of participation and involvement. What these models lack, however, is the systematic analysis of power that Carr (2004) suggested was central to current initiatives around participation and involvement. In Chapter 2 we pointed out how Lukes (1974) has suggested that power needs to be understood in three ways: as the capacity to act (A having the power to make B do something against their wishes); as the management of dissent by the prevention of issues being placed on the public agenda; and finally by the lack of recognition on the part of powerless groups that their interests are being threatened (Lukes,1974; Hindess, 1996).

While this discussion takes us further than the rather simplistic analyses of power put forward by Arnstein and Alinsky, there is still a danger that we produce an analysis which appears to suggest that service users are passive in the face of the institutional power of large social work or professional agencies. How do we assert the capacity of service users to take action to gain power rather than have power handed to them (which must in any case be an unlikely scenario)? We can do this by seeing service users as people with the capacity to bring about change not only in their own, individual circumstances, but in the broader institutions and structures against which they struggle. As we noted in Chapter 4, *empowerment is essentially a political strategy. It is a deliberate attempt to widen access to power* (Reynolds, 1996, p153).

To make involvement and participation real, we need to look not just at how power can be exercised but also at how it can be resisted. How can we develop strategies to promote meaningful change? Giddens' analysis of agency and structure can provide some pointers as to how this may occur. He refers to power as *the transformative capacity of human action* (Cassell 1993, p109). This, Giddens suggests, following Marx, is the key element in the notion of praxis. The creation of a radical practice, based on notions of overcoming oppression, tackling discrimination/oppression and the creation of new cooperative social relationships, is at the heart of any theory of social action. Similar ideas can also be seen in the writings of Gramsci and Freire and particularly in the former's idea of the 'organic intellectual', someone with an understanding of the need for change which derives from their own experience, and the latter's idea of conscientisation, the notion that when the person becomes aware of the way their oppression is determined they develop the capacity to take action to change their situation (Gramsci, 1972; Freire, 1974; Mayo, 1999).

Foucault (1980) points to the way in which power is localised, *dispersed, heteromorphous* and accompanied by *numerous phenomena, of inertia, displacement and resistance*, so that, *one should not assume a massive and primal condition of domination, a binary structure with 'dominators' on the one side and 'dominated' on the other* (p142). In fact, power should be viewed as a dynamic concept in which individuals *are always in the position of simultaneously undergoing and exercising . . . power [they] are the vehicles of power, not its application* (p98). Foucault suggests that *the mechanisms of power [need to be analysed] on the basis of daily struggles at grass roots level, among those whose fight was located in the fine meshes of the web of power* (p116). This is the agency that we are looking for, the sense that service users can resist and reframe their experience in a way that can change the way services are delivered. However, it is necessary to avoid an outcome in which the organisation benefits more than the service user. As Jordan noted, outcomes can be seen in significantly different ways:

> the agencies' goal is to get target groups to bear as much of the costs of social care as possible, without sacrifice of professional power or significant material resources; the groups' to gain relevant resources and influence policy.
>
> (Jordan, 1996, p185)

Can we therefore integrate these understandings into a framework for evaluating involvement and participation which reflects the complex power dynamics in current welfare practice? The above models can, taken together, begin to provide a framework that we can use to evaluate the real extent of service user involvement in the newly aligned services we have discussed in earlier chapters. An outline of how this may look is provided in Table 5.4.

Table 5.4 Measuring service user involvement

Level of control/ strength of participation	Motivation	Resources	Degree of mobilisation	Dynamics of participation	Type of activist
Citizen control	Very strong	Managed	Strong catalysts	Collective identity	**Campaigner**
Citizen participation	Strong	No drain on resources	Dependent on issue	Weaker collective identity, more individualistic	**Foot soldier Thinker rather than doer**
Citizen non-participation	Weak	Not significant factor	Weak	Follower rather than leader	**Habitual participant Marginal participant**

This still has the danger of presenting us with a static, rather than dynamic, understanding of how service users can exercise power to challenge and change the current configuration of welfare services. We therefore need to superimpose a further matrix on that present in Table 5.4. This would show Lukes' dimensions of power overlaying the left-hand column with the first dimension mirroring citizen control, the second participation and the third non-participation. This would allow us to argue that service users need to generate the capacity to make agencies and institutions react favourably to them (citizen control/capacity to act). Participation would occur where agencies were no longer able to manage dissent but had to put issues on their agenda (citizen participation/management of dissent). Non-participation would be overcome where service users recognised their interest and acted to have them met (non-participation/ ignorance of own wants).

Equally there is a need to identify why people act or fail to act to redress any disadvantage they experience. One way of understanding this is by returning to Giddens' concept of agency, or what Fook (1999) has characterised as *a sense of responsibility, of agency, an appreciation of how each player can act upon it to influence a situation* (p200). Central to this, Fook suggests, is the development of a consciousness, which can imagine another different way of doing things, a point similar to that attributed to Foucault at the beginning of the chapter (Foucault,1981). This may involve setting agendas for change, not just responding to the agenda of those with power (Campbell and Oliver, 1996) and developing new participatory organisations and practices which signify real and lasting change (Hardcastle, 2004). This would clearly illustrate Foucault's point about individuals simultaneously undergoing and exercising power and would help us understand the way power operates (Foucault, 1980).

This change in perspective could then suggest a model of involvement, which was multi-dimensional (see Table 5.5).

Table 5.5 Power, participation and involvement

Level of control/ strength of participation	Degree of power: Lukes	Degree of agency: Giddens, Foucault, Gramsci, Freire	Motivation	Resources	Degree of mobilisation	Dynamics of participation	Type of activist
Citizen control	Capacity to act	Strong ↑	Very strong ↑	Managed	Strong catalysts	Collective identity ↑	**Campaigner**
Citizen participation	Management of dissent	Medium ↑	Strong ↑	No drain on resources	Dependent on issue ← →	Weaker collective identity, more individualistic	**Foot soldier Thinker rather than doer**
Citizen non-participation	Lack of awareness	↓ Weak	↓ Weak	Not significant factor	↓ Weak	Follower rather than leader	**Habitual particpant Marginal participant**

This model would provide us with a way of measuring activity and recognising the capacity of service users to generate change at all levels. Foucault's discourse can then remind us to see power as a fragmented rather than monolithic process and therefore one amenable to influence and control at a grass-roots as well as a structural level. This may help us as welfare professionals to recognise that change is possible and may lift the sense of anxiety many welfare professionals express about their own lack of social and political power. We will return to these debates in later chapters.

ACTIVITY 5.6

Jo and Karen have lived together for the last ten years. Jo was a manager in an IT firm until he was forced to give up work because he began suffering from severe reactive depression. Karen is wheelchair bound following a road accident and she is paralysed from the waist down. They both attend the local community centre.

Karen has been approached by her social worker to become a member of the local Disability Information Forum. This meets monthly with professionals from social services, health, the Department of Work and Pensions and the university. The group makes representations to the local services about how disability services are run. There are two service users with disabilities and two carers represented on the committee. The other 12 places are made up of local professionals. They want Karen to replace a service user representative who is standing down. She will not receive any expenses but will have travel provided. Jo was also interested but there is only one place available.

This is a chance for Karen to influence how services are developed and she is keen to be involved. Karen is considering joining the Forum.

- *what issues should she bear in mind when making her decision?*
- *Are there any barriers to her involvement?*

ACTIVITY 5.6 *continued*

- *If so, how could they be overcome?*
- *Using Arnstein's ladder of participation how would you evaluate Karen's involvement?*
- *Can Karen ensure her voice is heard; if so, how?*

Comment

The material provided above should allow you to assess the efficacy of Karen's involvement and the likelihood that she can make an effective contribution to the organisation.

CHAPTER SUMMARY

This chapter has looked at the way in which the involvement of service users/carers has become part of mainstream policy development within UK social work. It traced the development of service user involvement and demonstrated how it has come to play a central role in current policy development. It pointed to the way recent policies from *Valuing people* to *Independence, wellbeing and choice* have placed a greater emphasis on service user/carer involvement. In most current policy discourse the focus is on issues such as choice, independence and dignity and new forms of practice which incorporate these principles (see the discussion of pedagogy in the following chapters).

The chapter asked whether this sense of involvement was real or tokenistic, merely a platitude or evidence of real commitment to make services that people use accountable and responsive to people's needs. Using as a starting point Arnstein's ladder of citizen participation the chapter then went on to develop a model for evaluating service user/carers' involvement which integrated notions of power and empowerment within a framework which explicitly evaluated the quality and impact of such involvement strategies. Drawing on European research around involvement it concluded that a multi-dimensional model of involvement should be constructed. It ended by suggesting a model of participation which acknowledged the importance of power relationships and reflected a commitment to developing an approach which placed service users at the heart of any participatory framework.

FURTHER READING

Arnstein, S (1969) A ladder of citizen participation. *Journal of the American Institute of Planners*, 35 (4), 214–24.
Classic text which outlines a model of citizen involvement which has been hugely influential since its publication almost 40 years ago.

Evers, A (2004) *Current strands in debating user involvement in social services*, Brussels: Council of Europe (downloaded from **www.coe.int/T/E/Social_cohesion/Social_Policies/04.activities**).
Report of research commissioned by the Council of Europe into trends in service user involvement in Europe.

Foucault, M (1980) *Power/knowledge: Selected interviews and other writings*. Brighton: Harvester.
Most accessible collection of writings of Michel Foucault, organised into key themes and including some of his most influential writing on power.

Heikkila, M and Julkunen, I (2003) *Obstacles to an increased user involvement in social services*. Strasbourg: Council of Europe.

Looks at the possiblities and constraints on service user involvement, drawing on a wide range of European examples.

www.coe.int/T/E/Social_cohesion/Social_Policies/04.Activities/1.Access_to-soc

http://scie-socialcareonline.uk

Chapter 6

New forms of practice: Professionalism, partnerships and pedagogy

ACHIEVING A SOCIAL WORK DEGREE

This chapter will help you begin to meet the following National Occupational Standards for social work.

Key Role 1: Prepare for and work with individuals, families, carers, groups and communities to assess their needs and circumstances.
- Liaise with others to access additional information that can inform initial contact and involvement.

Key Role 2: Plan, carry out, review and evaluate social work practice, with individuals, families, carers, groups, communities and other professionals.
- Develop and maintain relationships with individuals, families, carers, groups, communities and others.
- Carry out your own responsibilities and monitor, coordinate and support the actions of others involved in implementing the plans.
- Examine with individuals, families, carers, groups, communities and others, support networks which can be accessed and developed.
- Work with individuals, families, carers, groups, communities and others, to initiate and sustain support networks.

Key Role 3: Support individuals to represent their needs, views and circumstances.
- Advocate for, and with, individuals, families, carers, groups and communities.
- Present evidence to, and help individuals, families, carers, groups and communities to select the best form of representation for decision-making forums.
- Enable individuals, families, carers, groups and communities to be involved in decision-making forums.

Key Role 5: Manage and be accountable, with supervision and support for your own social work practice within your organisation.
- Carry out duties using accountable professional judgement and knowledge-based social work practice.
- Contribute to monitoring the quality of the services provided.
- Share records with individuals, families, carers, groups and communities.
- Work within multi-disciplinary and multi-organisational teams, networks and systems.
- Deal constructively with disagreements and conflict within relationships.

Key Role 6: Demonstrate professional competence in social work practice.
- Work within the principles and values underpinning social work practice.
- Use professional assertiveness to justify decisions and uphold professional social work practices, values and ethics.
- Devise strategies to deal with ethical issues, dilemmas and conflicts.
- Contribute to policy review and development.

QAA Benchmarking Statement

1.10 Contemporary social work commonly takes place in an inter-agency context, and social workers habitually work collaboratively with others towards inter-disciplinary and cross-professional objectives. Honours degree programmes should, therefore, be designed to help equip students with accurate knowledge about the respective responsibilities of social welfare agencies and acquire skills in effective collaborative practice between these.

National Occupational Standards for Community work

Key Role A: *Develop working relationships with communities and organisations.*

Key Role B1: *Contribute to the development of community groups/networks.*

B2: *Facilitate the development of community groups and networks.*

B3: *Facilitate ways of working collaboratively.*

B4: *Promote and support learning from practice and experience.*

B5: *Create opportunities for learning from practice and experience.*

Key Role D1: *Support communities to monitor and review action for change.*

D2: *Facilitate the development of evaluation networks.*

Key Role E1: *Encourage the best use of resources.*

E2: *Review and develop funding and resources.*

E3: *Develop and evaluate a funding/resourcing strategy.*

E4: *Develop people's skills and roles within community groups/networks.*

E7: *Develop and maintain organisational frameworks for community-based initiatives.*

Introduction

The last chapter illustrated how inclusion has become a key element of a new social work practice. This chapter looks at the other dimensions of the model outlined in the Introduction to this book – inter-profesionalism and internationalism. It draws attention to the centrality of power to discussions about the future of social work. It builds on earlier analyses by extending the discussion to encompass debates about professionalism and partnership. It shows how partnership can be facilitated and enhanced by utilising European models of social care and particularly social pedagogy.

Professionalism and power

Abbott and Wallace (1990) noted how the term 'professional' in modern society *is generally a term of approval and one that implies payment for special skills and proficiency. To claim to be a professional is to suggest independence, autonomy and control over work.* Typically, until fairly recently, social work has not been seen in this way. It has struggled on the margins of the professional project and social workers have often been seen at best as 'semi-professionals', defined by Toren (1969) as occupying that place where theoretical study is replaced *by the acquisition of technical skill. Technical practice and knowledge is the basis of semi-professions such as... social work* (p143).

However, critical and particularly feminist sociologists have pointed to how the existing professions are often structured by social division along gender and race. Hugman (1992) recognised how difficult it was for women to overcome gender division in the professions because of the way their experience was often individualised. Witz (1992, p68) pointed to the source of this gender division when she noted how *strategies of occupational closure aim for an occupational monopoly over the provision of certain skills and competencies.* The result was that people seeking to enter professions were subject to processes of exclusion, where the profession seeks to deny membership through the imposition of forms of rule and control; demarcationary strategies, where a hierarchy of professions was established where access to a 'higher' level profession was often denied to 'lower' level professions, and dual closure strategies could be present which prevented both upward and downward mobility.

Abbott and Wallace warned about the way the idea of professionalism is used to:

> *police the actions of those who lay claim to professional status, certain standards of performance and behaviour are expected of them, standards set in essence from outside the control of the profession itself. Groups who aspire to professional status are laying themselves open to be controlled by externally defined standards.*
>
> (p10)

Writers such as Witz (1993) and Hugman (1998, 2005) showed how these standards are often inimical to participative forms of practice and that professions often establish barriers to exclude people from their particular professional practice. Often these barriers reinforce processes of discrimination and oppression.

Where does this leave social work? Social workers have often complained about the lack of professional credibility they receive from other professions and the difficulty they have in being heard in inter-professional debates. Is this because of their perceived semi-professional status? Lord Laming was critical of social workers' lack of critical practice in his report on the Climbié case. Introducing his report into the death of Victoria Climbié he commented:

> *In the months which followed [her becoming known to services] Victoria was known to no fewer than four social services departments, three housing departments, two specialist child protection teams of the Metropolitan Police. Furthermore, she was admitted to two different hospitals because of concerns that she was being deliberately harmed and was referred to a specialist Children and Families Centre managed by the NSPCC. All of this between 26th April 1999 and 25th February 2000.*
>
> *What transpired during this period can only be described as a catalogue of administrative, managerial and professional failure by the services charged with her safety.*

As a consequence, one of his major recommendations was that social workers should be prepared to be more critical of other professionals and be able to challenge decision-making which is unclear and lacking in focus. Can an increase in social workers' professional power redress this imbalance and secure for social work the professional identity some within it crave or will it result in us replicating the power imbalances identified by writers such as Witz? Will we end up erecting our own exclusionary and demarcationary strategies, and if so, what are the implications of such developments for the anti-discriminatory/anti-oppressive practices which are at the centre of our core values?

As we saw in Chapter 5, Foucault (1980) can help provide an insight into this issue. He conceived of power being about the 'structure of actions' which bear on those who are free. Often power is unstable and reversible. He says that:

> *the exercise of power demands a degree of freedom among those being governed, it need not imply the removal of liberty. Where there is no possibility of resistance there can be no exercise of power. Power is of necessity fragmented and diffuse, but is no less important for that.*

What he means here is that power is never so all-embracing that it cannot be fought against and for us that must suggest that the negative outcomes of the struggle for professionalism identified above are not inevitable but can be resisted and potential alternative relationships between trained and untrained people, professionals and service users can be developed.

Biggs (1997) suggests that such conflicts may be the outcome of the uncertainty we experience in a post-modern society (Bauman, 2001). Professionalism may be a product of the kind of hierarchical certainties which were prevalent in an earlier era where identity was more fixed and sustainable while the demands of service users may reflect a breakdown in that certainty and the opening up of new possibilities for people to assert their identity. The disparity between professionalism and service user demands for their needs to be met may signal the beginning of different types of relationship. Seen in this context we need to be aware of the potential for inter-professional activity to become a means of 'fixing' these professional uncertainties in such a way that professional power becomes recentralised in the hands of professionals rather than decentralised to those who use services.

To explore some of these dilemmas around professionalism it is useful to look at current debates around partnership and pedagogy, each of which suggests some fruitful ways of taking the debate forward.

Partnership

Partnership has been suggested as a way of ensuring the better coordination of services since the modernisation agenda was introduced in 1998 (Department of Health, 1998). Often it is portrayed as being a partnership of unequals, with the more powerful sector, normally the statutory sector, being seen as dominant. It is assumed that partnership is desirable because it can:

- improve effectiveness;
- see service users and carers as a source of knowledge and understanding;
- ensure that the rights of service users and carers are central to decision-making;
- be part of the process of empowerment.

Thompson (2005) sees partnership as meaning:

> *working* with *clients, rather than doing things to or for them. It involves moving away from the outmoded view of social work as a form of 'social medicine' in which the expert social worker diagnoses the problem and*

prescribes a cure or treatment programme. This medical model is gradually being replaced by a partnership based approach.

(p123)

This partnership approach, he suggests, is characterised by:

- assessment being carried out in close cooperation with the individual;
- intervention involving parties working together to resolve or minimise problems;
- the situation being jointly reviewed and evaluated.

As an approach, partnership is characteristic of social work in a multitutude of contexts, professional and national. For example, moves toward partnership models can be seen in Ireland (Ferguson and Powell, 2002, p93), Northern Ireland (Campbell and McColgan, 2002, p115), Wales (Doel and Williams, 2002) and England (Children Act 1989; Health and Social Care Act, 2004; Department of Health, 2006). The National Strategic Partnership Forum (a group bringing together 35 voluntary sector organisations, campaigning charities and primary care trusts) produced a paper in 2006 indicating how the third sector (see Chapter 4) could take forward the commitment to partnership contained in *Our health, our care, our say*. It concluded that joint working could benefit all sectors by ensuring that partnership arrangements included the following:

- *Strong user and care involvement.*
- *Community engagement.*
- *Access to hard-to-reach groups.*
- *Innovation.*

(National Strategic Partnership Forum, 2006, p17)

Often the idea of partnership is linked with other concerns about collaborative working, joint working or working together. Quinney (2006) points out how, while collaborative working is not new to the social work agenda, it has:

been widely promoted as a solution for addressing shortcomings and failures in public services, including the social work, health, education, youth work and housing services. There is now a focus on modern, seamless and personalised public services ... that seek to meet the increasingly complex needs of service users and carers though a rethinking of the policies, structures and professionals involved.

(p22; emphasis in original)

Quinney quotes Whittington (2003), who suggests that working in partnership can mean:

- *Working together to ensure joined up services.*
- *Meeting service user needs through providing services through more than one organisation.*
- *The nature of the relationships between service provider and service user.*

(Quinney, 2006:her italics, p11)

Quinney then suggests the following definition, again quoting Whittington:

partnership is a state of relationships, at organisational, group, professional or inter-professional level, to be achieved, maintained and reviewed; and collaboration is an active process of partnership in action.

(Whittington, 2003, p16)

Partnership or collaborative working can therefore take many forms.

- Multi-disciplinary teams – teams which comprise a range of professionals from different disciplines or specialisms, e.g. community mental health teams.

- Inter-agency working – situations in which different agencies participate to achieve a particular goal but which do not necessarily involve ongoing joint work or the relative dissolution of professional boundaries.

- Inter-professional collaboration – those occasions on which two or more professionals from different disciplines or specialisms work together to achieve a joint goal. This may not necessarily involve inter-agency collaboration but may involve intra-agency collaboration in which, for example, social workers and teachers employed by the same children's trust may work together on a common project.

- Common learning – the process through which professionals or trainee professionals from a diverse range of backgrounds come together to share learning in a common learning environment.

- Networks of organisations – those situations in whicn organisations come together in a formal network to achieve a common purpose, for example the Law Centres Federation, councils of community service, homelessness forums.

- Participatory relationships between professionals and service users – those situations where service users/carers work in an open and accountable way with professionals so that they have an equal relationship and through which the service user/carer is able to freely express their views and aspirations.

- Networks of service users/carers – formal or informal networks which are typically service user-led and which seek to advance the role of service users within a participatory framework which promotes democratic decision-making and engagement.

Power is a key determining factor in assessing the degree of partnership professions engage with. The above list provides a descending order of involvement and real partnerships. The partnerships at the top of the list are functions of improvements in service delivery and could be said to be consistent with Laming's requirement that agencies work together more closely. However, that does not disturb the power imbalance identified by Biggs (1997) in the inter-professional agenda – where do service users/carers feature in this integrated environment? As we noted earlier, Lukes (1972) suggested that power has three ways of manifesting itself. All three elements of power relationships are evident in debates around professionalism. The professional/service user relationship is often characterised (or constrained?) by the statutory power vested in social workers, particularly around child protection and work with people in mental distress. In itself this raises issues of whether social workers' primary responsibility is to control or empower service users (Hatton and Nugent, 1993; Baistow, 1994). Equally, while many situations require service user/family/carer input, often these interventions (case reviews, child protection conferences, mental health reviews) are structured by the professional, and the service user's input is to comment on rather than set the agenda. Finally, professional ideology invests in the professional an expert status which values their views while marginalising those of the service user. This process seeks to encourage people using services to believe that decisions made are in their interests, while masking the power relationships between provider and user. To some extent good anti-oppressive practice should minimise or reduce these power imbalances yet there is a danger that the full onset of social work's professional identity will push us back toward the idea of controlling the behaviour of the people with whom we work rather than reasserting the commitment to empowerment which the more radical social work traditions discussed in earlier chapters would suggest is the way forward.

Making partnerships relevant and meaningful is therefore dependent on a number of factors, including:

- ensuring that partnerships are real and not tokenistic;
- building-in appropriate evaluation strategies to ensure that this is true;
- avoiding tokenism;
- learning from the experience of people pursuing different approaches, sometimes in other countries.

A number of these issues are addressed more fully in Chapter 5.

ACTIVITY *6.1*

- *What does the definition of power presented above tell us about partnership?*
- *Can it suggest something about the way service providers and service users work together?*
- *Which model of partnership makes the issue of power clearer?*

Comment

To undertake this exercise see the sections on Lukes and Foucault in this chapter and Chapter 5. You will also need to look at the implications of the Climbié enquiry.

Partnerships in practice

It may help clarify these issues if we examine some ways in which partnership can be observed in practice settings. The first example is taken from the New Generation Project, a collaboration between the Universities of Portsmouth and Southampton to deliver inter-professional teaching to students. The second looks at a practice-based partnership between agencies and educational institutions to deliver training and education to the social care workforce (Hants/Isle of Wight Learning Resource Network).

CASE STUDY

New Generation Project (NGP) – Universities of Portsmouth and Southampton

This is an inter-professional common learning project, funded by the Department of Health and jointly provided by the Universities of Portsmouth and Southampton, initially with support from the Hampshire and Isle of Wight Workforce Development Confederation. It seeks to provide common learning for pre-qualifying professionals in a range of disciplines – social work, nursing, diagnostic and therapeutic radiography, pharmacy, audiology, podiatry, medicine, physiotherapy and occupational therapy – through problem-based learning in small inter-professional learning groups. These groups are facilitated by academic staff at the two universities and the project seeks to provide focused learning for students from across the professions.

Integration into Curricula *The two universities sought to make the most of their involvement in the NGP to facilitate and enhance the quality of the students' learning experience by arranging additional teaching support for the programme. At present this involves:*

- *a designated member of staff carrying out preparatory teaching around NGP prior to the students undertaking the IPL (Inter-Professional Learning) units at levels 1, 2 and 3*

- *an introduction to the way ILP impacts on the students' learning experience while on work placement at levels 2 and 3.*

Students also use these sessions to raise issues directly with the lecturer taking the session.

The staff and student group are committed to inter-professional and collaborative working and the social work students are seeking to make the NGP even more relevant to social work training by expanding the range of professions involved to include professions with a closer working relationship with social work such as probation/ criminal justice, youth offending teams, education and schools. It is anticipated that this will make the NGP more responsive to social work's concerns and more relevant to students' practice. Portsmouth has throughout sought to deal openly with its student group, to listen to and value their comments and where appropriate to raise issues either with the NGP or within the university. The student experience will continue to be at the centre of this initiative, thus ensuring that students continue to experience a high quality programme.

Example of IPL unit at level 1 *This is a brief outline of the IPL level 1 unit of the New Generation Project. Its focus is on encouraging students to understand each other's roles, the development of appropriate methods of communication and the development of skills in critical and reflective practice.*

Aim
To introduce students to collaborative learning and team working.

CASE STUDY *continued*

Learning outcomes

On successful completion of this unit, students should be able to:

1. *describe team roles and strategies for team working;*
2. *meet their obligations to others in the learning group through their participation in collaborative learning, including using an electronic forum;*
3. *explain the roles and responsibilities of the different professions represented in their IPL group;*
4. *begin to reflect on their own views and expectations of professionals' roles;*
5. *communicate in an appropriate style for group processes and team working;*
6. *access, evaluate, select and share information from a range of sources.*

The syllabus   The topics covered in the unit include: adult learning; collaborative learning; communication; giving and receiving feedback; group dynamics; health and social care teams; health and social care trends and issues; learning styles (Honey and Mumford); professional roles and stereotypes; reflection; strategies for effective team working; team roles (e.g. Belbin, 1981); analysis and selection of health and social care information.

An example of an inter-professional learning opportunity is the first exercise the students undertake. This introduces the concept and practice of collaborative learning and team working and involves the students:

- *participating in a discovery trail set in a geographical area of Portsmouth or Southampton;*
- *exploring effective team working;*
- *considering the process of reflection;*
- *researching their health and social care professions.*

This is followed by a further week in which students explore collaborative learning online. During this week students will explore a scenario and review the different professions' contributions to the client/s/patient/s in the scenario and identify where inter-professional teamwork would improve the client/patient experience.

The NGP is currently undergoing an extensive evaluation for the Department of Health and a five-year evaluative report should be available in 2008/9. However, some of the key actors contributed to an initial analysis of the programme in 2006. At that time the programme had a total of 1,394 students from the professional programmes mentioned above. O'Halloran *et al*. (2006) argue that the model of learning is based on collaborative inter-professional learning and consists of three pedagogies: guided discovery learning; collaborative learning and inter-profesional learning. These pedagogies they define as being characterised by the following:

- **Guided discovery learning**   which they describe as 'learning how to learn' through the *process of discovery and the exploration of knowledge coupled with the responsibility to master the content needed for understanding* (p18). Learning is achieved here through encouraging students to develop a learning portfolio.

- **Collaborative learning** quoting Koehn (2001, p160), they describe this as an *intellectual endeavour in which individuals act jointly with others to become knowledgeable on some particular subject matter* (quoted in O'Halloran *et al.*, 2006, p180). Central to this is cooperation among the student group to achieve joint learning objectives.

- **Inter-profesional learning** is characterised by processes of learning with and about one another.

The interaction of these three pedagogies, it is hoped, will help students achieve a degree of mutual understanding and respect which uni-professional education is unlikely to be able to replicate. While the outcome of the longitutidinal study of the programme being undertaken is awaited, the authors point to the success of the programme in achieving *attitudinal and knowledge change in students over the duration of common learning and into practice* (O'Halloran *et al.*, 2006, p26). The anecdotal evidence from students on the IPL programme is that levels of mutual understanding and respect among the professions undertaking the programme increases exponentially throughout the programme. By level 3 students are talking much more clearly about the advantages and potential pitfalls in inter-professional working. It remains to be seen whether this translates into social work students eventually becoming the kind of critical professionals envisaged by Laming but it at least provides a possible model for future professional development.

(The New Generation Project Longitudinal Study is available at: http://eprints.soton. ac.uk/16217)

Learning resource networks

The second type of partnership refers to the way social work agencies and educational institutions are working together to improve the experience for qualifying social workers. The mechanism for achieving this is through the development of learning resource networks (LRNs). These were established in the first instance to support the development of practice learning opportunities (work placements) for the new degree in social work which was introduced in 2003. The degree was seen as an attempt to improve the professional standing of social work *vis-à-vis* other similar professions such as nursing and teaching by introducing an extended period of training (from two to three years) and regulating and credentialising the profession. A new regulatory body, the General Social Care Council, had been established to oversee the change and to introduce procedures for registration of all professionals wishing to use the title 'social worker' (see Horner, 2006, pp117–20). (These changes therefore move social work toward a more established professional identity and raise within them some of the key issues discussed above.)

The LRNs were established initially to *increase the quality, quantity and diversity of practice learning opportunities (PLOs) for students* on such training courses (Skills for Care, 2006, p8). The LRNs were organised on a regional basis and were formed from partnerships of social care employers (statutory agencies such as local authorities, voluntary and independent-sector agencies), local universities and other education providers and bodies such as the Workforce Development Directorate and the Learning and Skills Council. Initially they were meant to focus on ensuring that sufficient practice learning opportunities existed for the new social work degree (which had a much larger placement element to it – 200 days over the three years of the degree compared with 130 days over two years under the Diploma in Social Work). However, it was then expected to roll out to the wider social care workforce, focusing particularly on providing training opportunities for the unqualified workforce which, as we saw in Chapter 1 was the vast majority of people working in social care.

CASE STUDY

The Hants/Isle of Wight Learning Resource Network

The Hants/IOW LRN is an example of such developments. It is jointly chaired by Hampshire County Council and the University of Portsmouth, (Head of Centre for Social Work). The Hants/IOW LRN came together in September 2004 to promote joint initiatives around the new Social work degree and the wider social care workforce. The LRN (previously LRCN) was initially funded by TOPSS England and is now funded by Skills for Care England through its Southern Region. The Hants/IOW LRN is one of four in the Southern Region – the others being Thames Valley, Sussex/Surrey and Kent/Medway.

During 2004/5 the major part of the Hants/IOW's agenda concerned developing placement opportunities for the new social work degree. This was most clearly represented by the 'Promoting Innovations in Practice' conference held at the Rosebowl in Southampton in November 2005, which attracted speakers from the Department of Health and over 180 delegates from local agencies and HEIs.

In 2005/6 the Hants/IOW LRN had a total budget of approximately £260,000 which it used to fund a number of important initiatives, including the following.

- *Promoting innovative placement opportunities such as student units and partnerships between local authorities and voluntary agencies, e.g. Motiv8 and the partnership between Southampton City Council and Southampton Solent University.*

- *Developing initiatives to promote service user involvement, including*
  - *mapping service user and carer involvement in social work education;*
  - *developing service user/carer involvement in the LRN;*
  - *developing training for service users/carers to audit potential placements;*
  - *developing new practice learning opportunities in small user/carer-led organisations. (The last two contracts were awarded to the Service User Inclusion Group at the university.)*

- *Providing funding to facilitate student placements on the Isle of Wight, particularly in respect of travel and accommodation costs.*

- *Employing a project manager and project development officer to promote the work of the LRN, liaise with other parts of the region and participate in national developments.*

- *To develop a comprehensive sub-regional plan to deliver social work education and training and ensure that resources in the sub-region are maximised by reducing the need for competition between HEIs and between employers. The LRN's key theme is* Collaboration not Competition, *which is meant to represent the best form of partnership in which the interests of the whole are greater than that of any of the individual parts.*

This budget was severely curtailed in the next financial year (2006/7) and a number of these developments were unlikely to continue over the next year, even as the LRN broaden its agenda to include the wider social care workforce.

The LRNs nationally were based on a philosophy described by Took (2006) as including the following:

- Early thinking
  - support for practice learning development;
  - extending role to support all social care training activity.

- Wider possibilities in development
  - people who use services and informal carers;
  - information and resource bank (SCIE connection);
  - PQ and continuing professional development – with the S4C/CWDC regional PQ planners.

- And for the future
  - wider workforce planning and development.

Took pointed to the importance of this initiative when he drew attention to the size of the current social care workforce. As can be seen in Figure 6.1, social workers (column two) are only a small part of the total workforce.

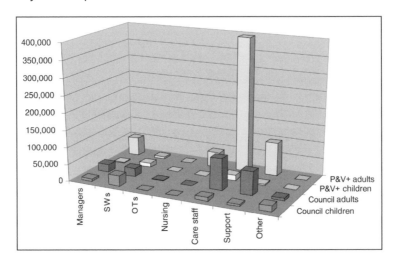

Figure 6.1 Social care workforce (from Took, 2006)

As can be seen from Figure 6.1, social work is only a small part of this agenda which includes the training needs of a wide variety of staff across the social care workforce, which the Department of Health estimates as being in the region of 924,000.

Indeed, Lionel Took suggested at the Promoting innovations in practice conference in November 2005 that future training priorities would include:

- improved opportunities for progression from social care into nursing and social work professional training;
- elearning programmes;
- the development of a comprehensive competence framework and National Occupational Standards;
- more NVQ training;
- inspection of training providers.

Took also suggested the likelihood of changes in service formation, which might include improved integrated local partnership working:

- community development;
- prevention, enablement and early intervention services;
- support and care services.

The focus here is on developing approaches to partnership working which promote community involvement, focus on prevention and early intervention, and provide appropriate and focused support and care services to meet the needs of a diverse population. To achieve this, he suggested, there was a need to create new models of service delivery which could include:

- extra care housing;
- homeshare;
- adult placement;
- technology-enabled services – assistive technology;
- connected care centres.

These changes, if introduced (and they map against those suggested in *Our health, our care, our say* and *Every child matters*), will push social work even further toward partnership work. The question of which partnership model we seek to adopt will then be of more than academic interest and could well impact on the future direction social work takes and in particular its ability to maintain its commitment to humanistic and anti-oppressive principles. This is of particular concern because, of the partnership models delineated above, the Department of Health's agenda fits much more closely with those that support the enhancement of professional power than those seeking to promote service user empowerment.

Other types of partnership

As we have seen, partnership is an elastic concept which can encompass a wide variety of relationships. Other examples for instance could include the following.

Partnerships in research

An example is the Homelessness Action Research Team, which is a partnership to identify the needs of the street homeless between:

- local homelessness agencies;
- ex-street homeless;
- police;
- a local hospital's accident and emergency department;
- a university.

The group produced a piece of action research, 'No place to go', which highlighted the need for new types of services for street homeless people within the Portsmouth area.

International partnerships

These may take a variety of different forms, including:

- issue-driven partnerships – FEANTSA (European Observatory on Homelessness, partly funded by the European Union, Disabled People's International);
- politically driven – anti-globalisation movement and globalisation from below;
- educationally driven – between universities to deliver collaborative programmes which develop programmes across specialisms – for example, European masters' programmes which bring together universities from across Europe.

The future development of these approaches seems assured. The recent *Options for excellence review*, which grew out of the discussions following *Our health, our care, our say* and *Every child matters* (see Chapter 1), suggests that one of the ways in which the workforce can be modelled around new ways of working lies in the establishment of common standards for inter-agency working. These standards will reflect changes in the delivery of social work services within the UK but will also need to be consistent with proposals coming out of the Department of Health and the Department for Education and Skills for the workforce, particularly in children's services, to learn from the experience of European colleagues who have been using a pedagogic approach to deliver a highly qualified and flexible workforce.

Pedagogy

Pedagogy or social pedagogy is a European social work tradition which, although referenced by writers as early as the 1980s (Davies, 1984) or more particularly the 1990s (Berry, Cannan and Lyons, 1992; Lorenz, 1994), has only recently begun achieving attention within the UK, specifically as a way of meeting the training needs of that part of the social care workforce in residential settings, where the levels of qualification are way below those found in Europe.

Petrie (2003) has written about how 'pedagogy' can be rendered invisible through the process of translation, as its most obvious translation is as education, and pedagogues therefore appear as teachers. While there is undoubtedly an element of education in pedagogy, it seems more useful to see the concept as one which can inform the practice of social professionals. As Petrie notes:

> *the whole domain of social responsibility for children, for their well being, learning and competence . . . the use of the term pedagogy allows for a discourse that can arise above differences based on for example, the age of those who use services or a service's immediate goals; it permits any particular provision to be located in the context of a wider social policy towards children.*
>
> (Petrie, 2003, p13)

Hamalainen (2003) says that social pedagogy has a wide range of uses as an approach in social work, because it:

> *Concentrates on questions of the integration of the individual in society, both in theory and in practice. It aims to alleviate social exclusion. It deals with the processes of human growth that tie people to the systems, institutions and communities that are important to their well-being and life management. The basic idea of social pedagogy is to promote people's social functioning, inclusion, participation, social identity and social competence as members of society.*
>
> (Hamalainen, 2003, p76)

Elsewhere Petrie describes pedagogy as person-centred – *head, hands and heart – all three being essential for the work of pedagogy* (Petrie, 2004, p4). She suggests that pedagogic training could usefully be incorporated into UK work with children, particularly looked-after children (Petrie, 2004; Boddy, *et al*., 2003).

As can be seen from the above, pedagogy has many elements to it and can be said to be influenced by a diverse range of theories from Kierkegaard to Freire to social constructionism (Burr, 1992; Hatton, 2001). Higham (2001) has suggested that pedagogy is rooted in humanistic principles, arguing that social pedagogy promotes well-being through broadly based educational activities . . . [and] prevents social problems by empowering people with knowledge and skills to manage their lives (Higham, 2001, p25). Clearly such an approach draws on Freirian ideas about 'conscientisation' (Freire, 1972; Popple, 1995; Mayo, 1999), particularly where Freire talks about the need for dialogue, deindividualisation and critical thinking (Freire, 1972; see Chapter 3).

What then is pedagogy? Lorenz says of the development of pedagogy in Germany:

> *The pedagogical emphasis on socialisation into a community . . . informed theories of social intervention promoting social skills and 'integration' . . . the radical critique of total institutions diverted pedagogical activities away from traditional settings (schools, homes, the family) and towards the complexity of everyday situations. Social learning and change can only occur through open communication and with full participation of the 'client' or 'learner', not under 'artificial' conditions controlled by the social worker or the agency.*
>
> (Lorenz, 1994, p96)

This suggests an approach which is much more grounded in the needs and aspirations of the people we work with and is in some way antithetical to any attempt to impose a new managerialism (Dominelli and Hoogvelt, 1996) into the relationship between people who use services and those who provide them. Can a focus on pedagogy allow us to reclaim some of the person-centred and humanistic approaches which have got lost in the new professional culture we are being asked to develop?

Reference to pedagogic approaches being pursued in Denmark may help answer the question. Two key ideas stand out from the pedagogic traditions adopted by colleagues in Copenhagen – the idea of the 'common third' and problem-based project work.

'Common third'

This is an idea which has not been widely explored in debates around the work of the social professions but which is used fairly widely within Danish pedagogy. Aabro describes the 'common third' as a descriptive project or ambition within the pedagogical tradition of relations in social work in which there is a *deliberate focus on the object as something outside the subject*, the object being a 'common thing' which 'both parts in the relation' can connect with. Husen describes this process as:

> To be sharing something, to have something in common, implies in principle to be equal, to be two (or more) individuals on equal terms, with equal rights and dignity (subject–subject relation). In a community you don't use or exploit the other (subject–object relation).
>
> (Husen, 1996, p231, translated by Aabro, 2004)

At the core of this relationship are notions of equality and respect and the eradication of unequal power relations. As Aabro suggests:

> through a common or joint activity the users and the social workers enter a subject–subject relation... [in which] the professional is meant to 'forget himself' and the things around him – and devote himself entirely to the process and activity... the pedagogical challenge is to be able to realise activities which don't reflect the interests and needs of only one part, but instead seek to establish a common and productive activity.
>
> (emphasis in original)

Lihme (2004) suggests that this relationship defines the social pedagogical approach as special because *in the work with the child, unlike therapy, is the perspective of 'action', better known as the 'common third', where social workers and children/young adults meet through a common potential of learning, on a basis of activity and action* (Lihme, p181, in Ritchie, 2004 – translation by Aabro, 2004).

Borghill, a student on the BA in European Social Work at Portsmouth during the academic year 2003/4, describes this process eloquently:

> The method involves pedagogues and service users concentrating on an activity together e.g. sports, repairing a car, or making a film, virtually anything. The point is that both the pedagogue and the service users have to be genuinely interested in the activity. This way their relation is moved to the

background and does not seem important anymore. They are working towards a common goal, which is meaningful to all participants.

The activity has to be seen as a whole process where the service users are involved as equals in all phases, which are: choosing the activity, planning how to carry it out, actually doing it and in the end appreciating the result and evaluating the process. The young people must be given responsibility and the possibility to use their potential. According to Husen this should strengthen the young person's self-confidence and identity and at the same time working together with other people requires social and communicative abilities such as understanding, cooperation and respect for the opinions of others and these skills will be developed.

(Borghill, 2004)

Problem-based project work

Problem-based project work has been a key element of pedagogical education in Denmark since the 1980s. Drawing on the work of critical theorists from within the Frankfurt School, the liberation pedagogy of Freire and the experiential-based learning of Piaget, a model known as the RUC model was *shaped as a combination of political and critical intentions and a learning theory that argued for the importance of student activity as opposed to blackboard activity* (Prins, 2004). Berthelsen, *et al.* define this approach as a:

pedagogical mode of study, where students – in cooperation with teachers and sometimes others – explore and deal with one or several problems closely related to the way in which the problems appear. This implies that the project work is to provide an ever stronger experience, more profound knowledge and a broadened perspective; that the problems are confronted and dealt with from different angles, free from the traditional subject borders, and that the choice of theories, methodologies and tools are linked directly to the choice of a problem. The role of the teacher is no longer only to provide knowledge, but also in solidarity with the students to work as inspirator, facilitator, supervisor, and consultant. The project work is concluded in a product which can be a report/paper, or be expressed through other medias or concrete actions.

(Berthelsen, et al.,1996, p23, translation by Prins, 2004)

Prins (2004) argues that this is consistent with the educational principles at Frobelse-minariat (the pedagogic institution at which she teaches) which focus on *how to enable students engage in empowering professional relations and thereby facilitate development in other people's lives. The ideal is self-reliant responsible social workers that are able to question their reality in a critical way and search for knowledge, understanding and solutions.*

Cameron, reviewing the implications of pedagogy for the UK, argues that pedagogy can be characterised as being about dialogue, relationships and the permission to take risks. Reviewing practice in residential care in Germany and Denmark, she suggests that it demands attention because of its focus on *the individuality of each resident and their circumstances* (Cameron, 2004, p143).

Cameron draws attention to the way pedagogy uses the heart, brains and hands in combination. Here 'heart' refers to the way pedagogues deal with the emotional demands of the job, *the need for warmth and compassion when doing . . . pedagogic or care work* (p145).

'Brains' refers to *an intuitive and a systematic synthesis of information, emotions and, critically, knowledge gained from study* (p145). While this undoubtedly accords with the pedagogic principles enunciated above, Cameron goes too far in asserting that pedagogy rejects universalist solutions in favour of a diversity of perspectives. Certainly in Denmark there is a tendency to place universalist principles at the core of social work/pedagogic interventions in a way that minimises difference (Hatton, 2001). However, she does suggest the importance of intuition in pedagogic practice, an approach which contrasts with the more managerial and outcome-based approaches discussed earlier. The 'hands' she suggested are represented through arts-and-crafts types of activities, although again this may be taken to infer a lower-key approach to that represented by those writers advocating the common third. However, this is consistent with the argument in earlier chapters (and the Conclusion) for an approach which emphasises creativity as a central concern of innovative practice. This can be seen in the development of creative partnerships within the youth service which encourage *new ways of thinking about learning that ha[ve] the relationship between individual learners, their local communities and creative practitioners at heart* (Miles, 2007, p274). The work of Eichstellar and Raper (2006) points to the connection between this approach and pedagogy, particularly when they refer to the way *pedagogy brings youth work back to its roots . . . pedagogy will force us to think about our respective roles and practices outside of our existing silos, and to share and combine our efforts* (pp7–8).

The attention afforded pedagogy in *Care matters*, *Youth matters* and recent output from the DfES and Department of Health (Boddy, *et al.*, 2005 – for which Cameron and colleagues in the Thomas Coram Unit must take a lot of credit) suggest that the principles underpinning pedagogy have been taken on board and are likely to provide significant challenges to the future direction of children's services in the UK. This research has resulted in calls for a new qualification built on pedagogic principles (Cameron, McQuail and Petrie, 2007). A recent review of youth services in a city in the south of England also mentions pedagogy on a number of occasions, welcoming *the likely future move towards a pedagogy-led approach* (Portsmouth City Council, Review of Youth Services, May 2007: section 5:27).

Clearly there are points of connection between the theories, principles and values underpinning both Danish and UK social work. The focus on equality, respect and student-centred learning is central to both traditions. It provides a means of focusing or refocusing social work on its humanist goals rather than the technocratic welfarism currently being promoted in the UK through the competency models favoured by bodies such as the General Social Care Council, Skills for Care and the Department of Health (Dominelli and Hoogvelt, 1996).

We can learn from these different theoretical approaches so that, as has been argued elsewhere, we can meet the challenge to *remain 'rooted' in our own understandings but be prepared to shift sufficiently...[so that] each other's contributions are respected while retaining a belief in the validity of our own contribution* (Hatton, 2001, p277).

The points of connection are highlighted in Table 6.1.

Table 6.1 Learning from each other

Country	Theory	Practice	Values
Denmark	Pedagogy: Common third Project-based project work	Empowering Promoting equality Risk promoting Sharing/enabling	Equality Respect Dignity Solidarity Humanism
UK (recognising the diversity of the UK particularly following devolution).	Person-centred, case management, residual progressive work in community	From individualistic, risk-minimisation casework to community development	Anti-discriminatory Promotion of difference Empowering humanism

The three key ways in which we can learn from pedagogic traditions can be summarised as follows.

Theory

Pedagogy reminds us of the need to focus on individual need, while providing a reference point in more collective models of service provision, particularly as found in many parts of Europe. It reminds of us of the importance of intuitive and not just evidence-based practice, and its emphasis on individual agency and understanding of broader social structures suggests a way of reconnecting social work to its more radical traditions (see Chapters 2 and 3). The UK emphasis on anti-oppressive/anti-discriminatory practice can, when integrated with this approach, provide a coherent theoretical approach which links together to provide a strategy for social change.

Practice

The trend toward managerialist approaches to social work has left many social workers in the UK feeling as if their training has been rendered irrelevant as the skills they are called on to use, at least in statutory settings, are much more procedural and instrumental than they would desire. Pedagogy and other European traditions can remind us of the importance of relationship work and of the need to promote rather than minimise risk (see Chapter 1). Ideas of empowerment, even if expressed differently, put the focus back on service users and provide an antidote to the perceived limitations in the care-management approach. The focus on collaborative working across professional settings can also promote the ideas of partnership and participation suggested in Chapters 5 and 6.

Values

A recognition of the importance of non-Anglo Saxon approaches to social work can also allow us to explore common ethical principles between our European partners and ourselves and can itself promote improvements in inter-cultural understanding and communication. Inter-cultural communication can promote the autonomy of different cultures within a framework which respects the way each culture is articulated and in turn can lead to inter-cultural action during which we can form inter-cultural relationships through which *we can ensure the need for common ground with the need to recognise difference* (Young, 1996, p209; Hatton, 2001). This in turn can improve our inter-cultural competence (Berry *et al.*, 2002). As social workers this will allow us to be receptive to the differing needs and aspirations of the people with whom we work and by bringing us into contact with people from other countries ensure a freshness in our approach to our own practice and the possibility that we can learn from each other in a way which respects each other's traditions. As the suggested elsewhere, it:

> may allow us to see the similarities as well as the differences between us, to recognize that truth does not reside in one set of culturally specific values but that ways of understanding, methods of working and commitments to social justice are often shared.

> (Hatton, 2001, p276)

This approach suggests the possibility of recapturing the focus of social work toward 'relationship' or 'preventative work' which have to some extent become marginalised in the UK, as evidenced by the discussions in Chapters 2 and 3. The focus on the 'common third' and 'problem-based' social work also suggests possible ways of forging partnerships which are more open, accountable and equal than those focused on eligibility criteria and 'risk minimisation' discussed in Chapters 1 and 5.

Pedagogy and social work training

The University of Portsmouth has been running a BA (Hons) European Social Work degree with a pedagogic seminarium in Copenhagen since 1992 (Brobeck and Horncastle, 1995; Hatton, 2006). It would have been easy for the university to impose a UK-centric approach to learning and to minimise the importance of pedagogic and androgogic traditions in other countries. In effect they could have been guilty of what Cornwell has called 'cultural colonisation' in that their methods were seen as intrinsically 'better' or more systematic than those found in other countries (Cornwell, 1994).

The university has attempted to overcome this problem by developing a joint curriculum and ensuring that the Danish approach to education was as fully reflected in the curriculum as the UK/US approaches. Consequently the international group-work and reflective review (based on the principles outlined above) in Copenhagen were given the same weighting as the more traditional academic approaches adopted in

Portsmouth. The programme is taught in English and this means that the responsibility for assessment lies disproportionately with the UK teaching team although as much assessment as possible is conducted jointly – for instance, UK tutors travel to Denmark for the international group-work presentations (social pedagogy and social care in Europe) and Danish tutors travel to the UK for the individual oral presentations (frameworks of comparison). This at least goes some way to meet the requirement that the programme has the:

> *flexiblity to incorporate each culture's (and subculture's) own methodologies*
> *of support . . . to focus on individual strengths and the structural*
> *(organizational, community, political) changes which can support and*
> *mobilize these strengths . . . [which] can be particularly useful for social work*
> *in an international context by virtue of its concentration on people's capacity*
> *to live in the face of seemingly overwhelming adversity.*
>
> (Taylor, 1999, p317)

One of the key challenges faced when establishing the BA European Social Work was that while the UK academics were all extremely well versed in the methodology, knowledge base and values underpinning UK social work, their knowledge of European traditions was much less developed. This was particularly true of pedagogy, a tradition which had received little exposure in the UK other than through the work of Hadyn Davies Jones (and initially this was available in Danish rather than English; Coutioux, *et al.*, 1984). It is easy to underestimate the lack of contact between UK and European traditions in social work, especially since the concept of pedagogy has become more widely known over the last few years (Higham, 2001; Boddy, et al., 2003; Petrie, 2004).

The experience on the Portsmouth programme is that pedagogy is used much more widely than purely a narrow, child-centred approach. In Denmark pedagogues are employed to work in residential and day-care settings, as part of multi-disciplinary teams (often with psychologists, social advisers and health workers; Harder, 1998) and in initiatives such as the SSP projects (social services, school and police, e.g. Blaeksprutten in Copenhagen). However, it is undoubtedly true that pedagogy can make a real difference to current UK thinking about social work, both in terms of values and the theories underpinning practice (Hatton, 2001).

Where does this leave us? We need to critically review our practice so that we are aware that:

- partnership is a complex term which can hide a wide variety of practice;
- professionalism, while providing us with status and recognition, can inhibit collaboration and be detrimental to service users/carers;
- pedagogy can remind us of the need to focus on relationship work and be less managerial in our practice;
- involvement is the key factor and this must be real, not tokenistic.

ACTIVITY **6.2**

Consider how the notion of partnership operates in either your placement agency or your employing agency.

- *Where does power lie?*
- *How involved are service users/experts by experience in decision-making?*
- *If the agency works with more than one profession, which partnership model best describes it?*
- *Does the involvement of more than one agency change the power relationships?*
- *Would the introduction of pedagogy have any impact on the agency? If so, what impact?*
- *How would a focus on intuition and relationship building change the practice you are currently involved with?*

Comment

This exercise is designed to enable you to think critically about the agency you work with. It focuses particularly on allowing you the opportunity to critically examine what partnership means. Many government publications from the *Modernisation* White Paper onwards and even before through initiatives such as *Working together* (1995) have enjoined social workers to work in partnership. Often this is seen as a good thing in itself, without any thought being given to the power imbalances at the heart of much partnership work. This is not to suggest that we should not work collaboratively; just that we should seek to understand the relationships underpinning such partnerships.

C H A P T E R   S U M M A R Y

This chapter has focused on new forms of practice and has, in particular, developed two of the book's key themes; inter-professionalism and internationalism. It began by looking at how social work has moved towards securing for itself professional status through enhanced levels of training, registration and a commitment to continuous professional development. It then looked at how notions of partnership and collaborative working could enhance the practice of social workers by ensuring that the interventions of social workers and other professional groupings were more focused and relevant to contemporary challenges. It explored the examples of an inter-professional education initiative, supported by the Department of Health, the New Generation Project, and an initiative to improve collaboration between educational and workforce providers, the Learning Resource Networks.

Finally the chapter looked at how European models of care were coming to influence current practice. It outlined the key elements of an approach common in continental Europe – pedagogy. It identifies the common principles underpinning such an approach – the common third and problem-based groupwork – and examines the way in which such an approach calls on a range of skills from the heart, brain and hands to achieve its goals. The chapter ends with a brief discussion as to how the goals of pedagogy link to the theory, practice and value of social work. It suggests that there are clear points of connection between pedagogy and UK social work and suggests some ways in which discussions around pedagogy could be taken forward. The next chapter will look at some practical examples of how European social work can influence UK practice.

Cameron, C (2004) Social pedagogy and care: Danish and German practice in young people's residential care. *Journal of Social Work*, 4 (2), 133–51.

An early article from one of the key researchers, the Thomas Coram Research Unit. The article looks at the experience of pedagogy in Denmark and Germany and at the possible implications for UK residential services.

Cameron C, McQuail, S and Petrie, P (2007) *Implementing the social pedagogic approach for workforce training and education in England: a preliminary study.* London: Thomas Coram Research Unit, University of London/Cabinet Office/Department for Education and Skills.

The outcome of the TCRU research on pedagogy which looks particularly at the possible ways in which pedagogy could be implemented in the UK.

Hatton, K (2006) Europe and the undergraduate programme. In Lyons, K and Lawrence, S (eds) *Social work in Europe: educating for change*. Birmingham: BASW/Venture Press.

Looks at the experience of international collaboration between a UK university and a Danish seminarium. The book which it features in provides a good overview of developments in social education in Europe.

Quinney, A (2006) *Collaborative social work practice*. Exeter: Learning Matters.

A useful introduction to the principles underpinning collaborative work.

Chapter 7

Learning from Europe: Reflections on the challenges to social work in selected European countries

3.1.5 The nature of social work practice
- The integration of theoretical perspectives and evidence from international research into the design and implementation of effective social work intervention with a wide range of service users, carers and others.

This chapter will also begin to help you achieve the National Occupational Standards in Community Development

Key Role A: Develop working relationships with communities and organisations.

Key Role B1:   Contribute to the development of community groups/networks.

B2:   Facilitate the development of community groups and networks.

B3:   Facilitate ways of working collaboratively.

Key Role C1:   Work within communities to select options and make plans for collective action.

C2:   Contribute to collective action within a community.

C3:   Support communities to plan and take collective action.

C4:   Ensure community participation in planning and taking collective action.

Key Role D1:   Support communities to monitor and review action for change.

Key Role E4:   develop people's skills and roles within community groups/networks.

E5:   Facilitate the development of people and learning in communities.

E6:   Develop and review community based organisational structures.

E7:   Develop and maintain organisational frameworks for community based initiatives.

(PAULO, 2002 National Occupational Standards in Community Development Work, **www.fcdl.org.uk/publications/documents/nos/standards**, retrieved 5 July 2006)

Introduction

The key themes of this book have now emerged. Concerns around inclusion, inter-professionalism and internationalism can be seen to be at the heart of current discourses on social work practice. In the previous chapter we drew attention to the way European and/or international discourses of social work can throw a different light on UK practice and suggested a way in which we can integrate these approaches into our work. This chapter concentrates on these developments, and looks in more detail at specific examples of the social work or pedagogic experience. The chapter suggests, through a review of social work/pedagogic projects in Ireland, the Czech Republic and Denmark, issues about our current practice which will allow us to test and perhaps implement forms of practice which are consistent with social work's traditional concerns around prevention and empowerment.

UK and European social work

Lymbery *et al.* (2000, p279) suggested that UK social work is currently much more prescriptive and regulated than social work in other European countries, although these countries may be moving closer to the UK model. They argue that:

most nations have resisted the reductive power of the competence model and insisted on a broader definition of social work expertise ... it is not beyond the bounds of possibility that similar forms of regulation will start to take shape elsewhere. In that sense Britain could yet serve as an unwelcome model for the rest of Europe.

There is certainly some evidence that this development of a more regulated approach is happening in the Czech Republic. However, before looking at social work in Ireland, the Czech Republic and Denmark it is necessary to establish whether there is any such activity as a 'European' social work. Lorenz (1994) suggested that *regardless of the particular model of welfare state within which social work operates there are great similarities in the daily practice of social workers* (p28). He declined to define social work, arguing that *social work has a history of uncertainty and constantly changing identities* (p14). Munday (1996) described social work as a *notoriously difficult term to define, with significant variations across Europe in what constitutes a 'social worker'* (p7). Marynowicz-Hetka, Piekarski and Wagner (1999) suggest that:

> *the category of social professions includes both professionals, that is persons specially trained to work with specific types of persons, families, social groups and communities at high social risk, [and] persons who conduct this type of work as volunteers and have no professional training.*
>
> (1999, p23).

For the purpose of this discussion, we can define social work across Europe as a form of social professional activity which engages with people in a way that promotes their empowerment and aims to achieve a fair and more equitable society. It is beyond the scope of the book to develop a full comparative framework for evaluating social work across different countries and the reader is referred to other works which deal with these issues in far greater depth (Hokenstad and Midgley, 1997; Lyons, 1999; Adams, Erath and Shardlow, 2001; Healy, 2001). Within this context social professional activity should itself be seen in terms of the contribution we can make as change agents to igniting processes of social transformation. As such, social work shares professional concerns and dilemmas with a range of occupational groupings, including:

- *social pedagogues;*
- *social and special educators;*
- *agogues (community leaders);*
- *animateurs (a French profession focusing on young people's leisure activities);*
- *social workers;*
- *youth and community workers.*

(Lorenz et al., 1996)

Lyons argues that *a comparative approach can assist with the identification of common problems and provide encouragement for innovative practices* (Lyons, 1999, p159). She suggests that involvement with other social professionals can be an enriching experience and that it can raise awareness of the commonality of some basic human needs and problems, and of the cultural differences which influence their expression and the forms of societal and social responses. Erath, Hamalainen and Sing (2001, p3) suggest that comparative approaches to social work can:

Offer a medium through which social work may be reconnected with its primary concern in the alleviation of poverty, alienation and oppression and the promotion of human potential for developing both individual capacities and social environments.

This suggests that examining social work in other countries can reconnect us with the central themes of radical social and community work identified in Chapters 2 and 3. This analysis would suggest that social work in the UK and Europe shares common concerns, which while not exclusive to social work are central to the practice of most social workers and the experience of most people who use social services. What are these common problems? It is possible to identify a number of significant dilemmas facing social workers in Europe, including:

*   racism;
*   exclusion, marginalisation and poverty;
*   managerialism (see Chapter 1);
*   demands from service users (see Chapter 5);
*   Europeanisation and internationalisation (see below).

Racism

We noted in Chapter 3 how Lorenz pointed to the challenge racism posed for the social professions if we see them as part of the process through which are reproduced dominant discourses around power (see discussion of Foucault in Chapter 5). Lorenz suggested that racism was a major challenge for social work and that we need to demonstrate how discussions of racism are not just common-sense understandings of the world around us (it's natural to see people as different) but are the outcome of a discourse which promotes the aspirations of the minority population in a negative and demeaning way.

Speaking at the Ostrava Conference of ECSPRESS (the European Consortium of Social Professions with Educational and Social Studies) in 1998, he argued that *the role of the social professions in relation to the growing danger of exclusion and racism remains crucial for the achievement of a social Europe* (Lorenz, 1998, p5). He pointed to the way ECSPRESS was seeking to ensure that European integration *does not cause greater fragmentation and new forms of exclusion* (p3).

Despite this emphasis on a more politically active from of practice, social work in the UK is increasingly seen as a residual service meeting the needs of the poor and disadvantaged (Buckley, Skehill, and O'Sullivan, 1997; Davis and Wainwright, 2005). We saw in earlier chapters how social work can adapt to this kind of challenge because of its connection to the experience of people who use services and the commitment to accountability and inclusiveness which are at the centre of good social work practice.

Poverty, exclusion and marginalisation

We noted in earlier chapters how the particular discourses around poverty and exclusion can impact on practice. This remains important in any discussion of European social work. Poverty is an important issue across Europe (Gordon and Townsend, 2000) and as such impacts significantly on the people with whom social workers engage. Lister (1998, p29) sees poverty as spelling *exclusion from the full rights of citizenship in the social and civil spheres*. This exclusion is compounded by the way neo-liberal policies increasingly blame people in poverty for their circumstances and attempt to push social workers towards an individualised response to what is a structural problem (Dominelli, 2004; see discussion in Chapter 1). Writers such as Dominelli and Powell argue that this leads to a focus on managerialist responses to the problems facing service users and can result in a marginalisation of the concerns of the people using services in the face of an over-concern with managerial imperatives such as budgetary control, the development of restrictive criteria to govern eligibility for services, and a focus on professional concerns rather than social change perspectives. As a consequence some of the more innovative and radical approaches described earlier in the book can become marginalised (Penna, Paylor and Washington, 2000; Powell, 2001; Dominelli, 2004). This can lead to:

- the individualisation of service users' experience;
- a focus on crisis intervention rather than preventative work;
- social work being evaluated through measurable outcomes and the associated problem of prioritisation by eligibility criteria;
- social work becoming risk averse (see Introduction and Chapters 1, 5 and 6).

How can the negative connotations of such approaches be overcome? This may be achieved, for example, by the following:

- Increasing accountability. We have argued for greater service user involvement in service delivery and education, more democratic structures, and anti-discrimination (Chapter 5).

- New grassroots organisations – of Roma/Gypsies/Travellers, organisations of young people from BME groups, disability activists, social action projects. These are about reclaiming social work's radical roots (see Chapters 2 and 3).

- The development of new international lobbies – new organisations to replace ECSPRESS, IASSW and IFSW.

- Confronting the neo-liberal agenda and putting social work forward as an agency of change.

ACTIVITY 7.1

Either individually or in groups, consider the following:
- *In what way does poverty impact on people who use social work services in the UK?*

- *How can social workers engage with people experiencing racism?*

- *What implications do these issues have for current social work practice?*

Social exclusion: www.cabinetoffice.gov.uk/social_exclusion_task_force/
Neighbourhood renewal: www.neighbourhood.gov.uk

Comment

Use the material in this and earlier chapters to look at what poverty means and how it structures the lives of many people using social services within the UK (see Dominelli, 2004, pp34–9). For many people the experience of poverty is further exacerbated by the racism they experience within the UK (MacanGhaill, 1999). Use the National Occupational Standards for social and community work to look at which key roles a social worker would need to use to undertake practice which could incorporate a concern with poverty and racism.

Learning from a social pedagogic approach

We noted in Chapter 6 the way the European concept of pedagogy has begun to attract attention in the UK. A recent conference, 'What is pedagogy?', organised by the Thomas Coram Research Unit, brought together speakers and delegates from a number of European countries to look at how pedagogy could be introduced into social work in the UK. Hatton (2006) suggested that pedagogy can remind us of the need to focus on relationship work and be less managerial in our practice. As noted in Chapter 6, he argued that we can learn from pedagogic traditions in three key ways: theory, practice and values.

RESEARCH SUMMARY

Reviewing the use of pedagogy in residential child care services in Europe the Thomas Coram Research Unit (TCRU) identified the following key principles of pedagogic practice:

- *A focus on the child as a whole person, and support for the child's overall development.*
- *The practitioner seeing herself/himself as a person, in relationship with the child or young person.*
- *While they are together, children and staff are seen as inhabiting the same life space, not as existing in separate, hierarchical domains.*
- *As professionals, pedagogues are encouraged to constantly reflect on their practice and to apply both theoretical understandings and self-knowledge to their work and the sometimes challenging demands with which they are confronted.*
- *Pedagogues are also practical; their training prepares them to share in many aspects of children's daily lives, such as preparing meals and snacks, or making music and building kites.*
- *When working in group settings, children's associative life is seen as an important resource: workers should foster and make use of the group.*
- *Pedagogy builds on an understanding of children's rights that is not limited to procedural matters or legislated requirements.*
- *An emphasis on team work and on valuing the contributions of others in the task of 'bringing up' children: other professionals, members of the local community and, especially, parents.*

RESEARCH SUMMARY *continued*

- *Pedagogic theory is especially about relationships; child rearing to the pedagogue is essentially personal.*

- *It is a job where every day you must ask questions about yourself and your practice right to the end of your professional life. (French pedagogue working in a residential home, interviewed as part of TCRU's Social Pedagogy Study) (TCRU, 2003).*

ACTIVITY 7.2

In what way could pedagogy be used to change practice in the UK? Using the material in this chapter and Chapter 6 suggest three ways in which pedagogy could be utilised to improve social work practice with one of the key groups of service users.

Comment

You may wish to look at some of the more recent policy drivers which have included mention of pedagogy, including *Care matters* and *Youth matters*. The impetus for these developments has been concern at the poor experience of many young people in the looked-after system. Looking at the findings outlined above, how do they compare with the National Occupational Standards for social and community work?

Experiencing social and community work – reflections from Europe

The above discussion, and that in Chapter 6, provide a context for the following section. Here we look in more detail at the experience of social and community work of particular people in three European countries. In Ireland and the Czech Republic we look at the experience of a similar group – in Ireland, Travellers, and in the Czech Republic, the Roma. These groups have been specifically chosen because the work with which they engage touches on two of the book's key themes – inclusion and internationalism. However, they also throw light on the potential for people within these communities to discover solutions to their own problems and through this develop their own indigenous leadership. They therefore also allow us to reflect on the issues raised in Chapters 2 and 3.

The final discussion is more specifically about the experience of young people in Denmark and the way racism impacts on their lives. It looks at how pedagogues and social workers can work in a way which enables young people to overcome the racism they face. The remainder of this chapter draws on the author's experience teaching and researching in Ireland, the Czech Republic and Denmark. It looks specifically at projects which work with people excluded because of their race/ethnicity because given our commitment in the UK to anti-oppressive/anti-discriminatory practice it will allow us to focus on some of the lessons we can learn from attempts by excluded populations and the social workers/pedagogues with whom they work to develop their own solutions to the problems they face. Each section will provide a short overview of social work in that country before examining one project in greater detail.

Ireland and Irish Travellers

Background

Gilligan (1996) and Buckley *et al.* (1997) have pointed to the way in which the priorities for social work in Ireland have been largely determined by the state's response to disclosures of child abuse, particularly the Kilkenny Case (McGuiness, 1993). Ferguson (1996) suggests that, in the 1980s, the emergent childcare policy had largely been contained within the 'expert system', which ensured that *knowledge about child deaths and other organisational 'failures' continued to be institutionally repressed* (p25). This has been replaced more recently by a situation in which childcare discourse and practice has become politicised. Ferguson suggests that the debate on child protection has been reconstituted in two distinct ways. The role of the state has been more clearly articulated and the prevalence of a series of child abuse scandals and enquiries (McGuiness, 1993; Moore, 1995) has shown that *the safety of children cannot even be guaranteed by removing them from high risk home situations* (Ferguson, 1996, p27).

Skehill pointed to the contradictions between this regulatory and controlling framework and the attempts within the areas of community development and community action to engage with ideas of 'participation, empowerment and partnership' (Skehill, 1999, p177). In a more optimistic vein, Powell (1998) suggested that *the concept of empowerment and user rights . . . are seen as offering a new legitimacy to embattled welfare bureaucracies and professionals. The suggestion is that social workers, offering the quintessentially personal social services, can be pathfinders in this regard* (pp326–7). Elsewhere Powell (2001) has suggested the future of social work may well depend on how well it responds to such problems.

As we have seen earlier, this debate over the potential for social work to engage with processes of change is critical if we are to clearly map the way social work develops in the future. A good example of how people can engage with change processes is provided by looking at the experience of Travellers in Ireland.

Travellers have over the last ten to fifteen years begun to articulate their own demands for equality within the Irish state. The social and economic progress witnessed in Ireland during this period put the focus firmly on the way Ireland has failed to address the substantial levels of social inequality in Irish society (Nolan and Callan,1994; Callan, Nolan *et al.*,1996; Healy and Reynolds, 1998). The success of the 'Celtic tiger' resulted in growth rates of 7.5 per cent (among the highest in the world), low inflation and interest rates and increases in real living standards so that they became almost equal to EU averages (Sweeney, 1998). A national anti-poverty strategy (NAPS) was developed and the government introduced equality legislation prohibiting discrimination on the grounds of *gender, marital status, family status, sexual orientation, religion, age, disability, race and membership of the traveller community* (Equal Status Bill 1999; emphasis added).

This recognition of the need to tackle the disadvantage and discrimination facing Travellers is partly the outcome of a number of national commissions which have focused on the needs of Travellers (Commission on Itineracy 1963; Task Force on Travellers 1994), partly the outcome of work generated by the Combat Poverty Agency, a government-sponsored anti-poverty agency; and partly to the growth of an 'ethnic intelligensia' among Travellers (MacLaughlin, 1995). MacLaughlin argues that this is the outcome of developments within the Traveller movement but is also a response to *a virulent anti-Traveller Racism* and *the gradual internalisation of feelings of social inferiority among travellers themselves* (pp2–3). He suggests that the new leadership within the Travelling community has faced up to and struggled against this process of devaluing Traveller culture and life and has *politicised and radicalised Traveller issues* (pp82–3).

Ireland's history as effectively a British colony for much of the last 600 years has encouraged a belief that racism is something which happens to Irish people rather than a part of the experience of people within Ireland. Yet the experience of minority groups within Ireland, particularly the day-to-day experience of Travellers, provides substantial evidence that racism is deeply embedded in Irish social relations.

Aniagolu (1997) has argued that both the Irish people themselves and minority peoples within Ireland are guilty of *misrepresenting Ireland as a country free from racial prejudice*. Indeed *most Irish people still argue that the Irish are not racist* (p44). He suggests that on the contrary, Irish people were themselves implicated in racist oppression in many countries of the British Empire: *substantial numbers of Irish and Anglo-Irish people engaged in the slave trade and were actively involved in projects of colonial expansion* (p45). He points to the way in which racism in Ireland is constructed through people's own internalisation and replication of racist attitudes which they acquired from their colonisers through the process of colonisation.

Kensika Moshengwo of the Association of Refugees and Asylum Seekers in Ireland described how leaflets have been distributed in streets in the North Inner City and the West of Dublin inciting racial hatred and that these have been accompanied by physical attacks. He noted that *the physical abuse is directed almost exclusively towards blacks*. Pat Guerin of the Anti-Racist Campaign says *there is a perception among some local people that refugees are getting preferential treatment with regards to accommodation...a racially motivated murder is only a matter of time away*.

The tension exemplified by this comment typifies current debates in Ireland concerning asylum-seekers. Cullen (2000) noted that in Ireland, *official neglect of asylum-seekers over the past decade has wasted years of people's lives*. He pointed out particularly, and ironically given the history of Travellers in Ireland, that *when people complain in generalized terms about asylum-seekers, they are frequently talking about Roma* (p53).

MacLaughlin (1995) argued that the development of modern Ireland saw the creation of a politics of exclusion and a geography of closure which has *sought to exclude the foreigner from 'Fortress Ireland' and 'foreign practices' from Catholic nationalist Ireland* (p69). However, on the positive side the recommendations of the 1995 Task Force on Travellers prioritises Travellers' concerns and suggests a state commitment to tackling the discrimination they face. Perhaps more significantly this period *saw the emergence of an ethnic intelligentsia among the Travellers...[which] has contributed to the growth of an articulate leadership capable of voicing Traveller concerns and capable of raising the political consciousness of travelling people* (pp2–3).

Speaking at an international women's conference organised in Cork in 1993, Chrisie Ward, a Traveller, focused on the gendered inequalities faced by Travellers. She describes eloquently the hatred and discrimination which is both the historical legacy and current experience of Travellers and suggests that it is hardly surprising that younger Travellers react with anger to the discrimination they face. She says:

> *It is as if we are not as human as everybody else. We are seen as dirty, smelly, 'knackers'. It seems that the state can do what it likes with Travellers. This is because we are a minority. We are a small group on our own with no education. We know what we want but all we can use are our voices and our minds. This doesn't seem to have done us much good so far.*
>
> (Hyde, 1995, p64)

She concludes by arguing that Travellers need to organise themselves; they cannot or should not any longer rely on others to speak out for them: *Travellers need to stand up for themselves* (Hyde,1995, p63).

Helleiner argues that *anti-Traveller ideologies and actions have been linked to gendered constructions of Travellers* (p275). She suggests that:

> *the construction of domesticated Irish women in need of protection from a paternalistic state had implications for representations of Traveller women. However, this domesticisation of Travelling women and the gendered social relations incumbent on it was also reinforced within Traveller households. While Traveller women were important contributors to the household economy and possessed as a result a degree of autonomy other Irish women lacked, cultural practices such as restrictions on female sexuality before marriage and arranged marriages reduced their autonomy. Amongst Irish Travellers, as amongst the British Traveller-Gypsies, a controlled female sexuality was central to the ethnic self-definition while the settled women were attributed with uncontrolled sexuality.*
>
> (p282)

Travellers have begun, as MacLaughlin suggests to challenge these stereotypes. One Travelling woman said: *Travelling women have been very involved in community development because they have been involved in the issues.* Another said, *when we started off we were seen as troublemakers. I should have been home looking after my children. Corporations [local councils] saw us as frightening, not just as Travellers, we were women* (interviews with Travelling women 1998–2000).

Frazer (2001) has argued that community development has a key role in tackling racism in Ireland. The development of an autonomous Traveller movement with its own ethnic leadership will go a long way to creating the underpinnings for an equality agenda. The Gypsy/Roma community across Europe is developing much closer links and is also developing alliances with mainstream organisations within national and international contexts, including at a European level (McCann, 2000, pp174–6; see also the work of the European Roma Rights Centre).

Traveller Visibility Group

The new leadership is further exemplified by the Traveller Visibility Group (TVG), a Cork-based community development organisation which brings together Travellers and settled people in solidarity to facilitate community development work with the Travelling community. The TVG recognises Travellers as a *nomadic ethnic group with its own distinct culture and lifestyles* (Annual Report, 1997). Formed in 1992, the TVG aims to:

- promote Travellers as a nomadic group with its own distinctive culture and lifestyle;
- promote Traveller self-determination and empowerment;
- work for change and improvement in Travellers' lives including education, accommodation, health, employment and social rights;
- ensure the inclusion of Traveller issues and resource the real participation of Travellers in policy decisions and practices that affect their lives;
- promote mutual understanding, acceptance and support between Travellers and other groups in Irish society.

The TVG is therefore involved in a number of programmes to meet these aims, including:

- a Traveller Women's Community Education Programme;
- a programme promoting Travellers' health;
- the promotion of Traveller education and literacy;
- the promotion of Traveller inclusion through the enhancement of their involvement in the TVG;
- involvement in the National Traveller Women's Forum and the National Traveller Movement.

The TVG adopts a proactive approach in its work. One of the women in the project described how they began to tackle the discrimination they faced as Travellers:

TVG is in many ways unique. Previously work with Travellers had a very charitable approach. Charities were set up in all the counties. Some were very genuine but more were doing it for the power. In Cork a committee to help Travellers was set up but was not very effective. TVG started in late '92. We've run on a shoestring. We didn't have any funds. People were concerned about the conditions we lived in but they could not accept the conditions we lived in were caused by the political agendas going around us. We couldn't accept this, we split off. Travellers needed to be visible, that's why we call ourselves TVG. We look at the media and see how Travellers are visualised. We want to be visible in a positive way for positive reasons, to give Travellers something to celebrate. This community has faced oppression and marginalisation. It has inevitably become very isolated. We want to change that.

This comment and the above discussion illustrate the way even the most marginalised and disaffected groups of people have the capacity and ability to challenge discriminatory and oppressive legal and social processes. It clearly lends weight to the analysis in Chapters 2 and 3 of the potential people have to engage in progressive forms of practice. In particular it demonstrates the way that people can organise to form and control their own organisations and develop their leadership from within their communities.

Czech Republic: Integration or discrimination?

Background

Before 1989 the Czech Republic (then Czechoslovakia) was a centrally planned economy, with full employment and comprehensive social welfare for its citizens. After the Velvet Revolution (a relatively peaceful transfer of power from the old regime to a new government) in 1989 a number of key social policies were introduced to protect citizens from poverty. These included the development of the Existential Minimum (1991 – a social benefit introduced to secure a basic minimum income for those without access to other resources), a minimum wage, and a shift from social security (which was viewed as paternalistic) to social protection (which focused on individual need). Central to this new approach was the development of a 'social surviving net', a three-fold system involving social insurance, state social support and social assistance. This was established 1993 after the separation of the Czech Republic from Slovakia. The split with Slovakia led initially to a combination of a decrease in GDP, high rates of inflation, a fall in real household incomes, a drop in real wages, an increase in rental costs, cost of energy and travel costs (Chytil, 1998, pp48–9). Chytil suggests that the most significant factors characterising the new social arrangements were poverty, unemployment and crime.

- Poverty was previously related to family life cycle, but now a new form of poverty emerged characterised by unemployment, discrimination, the freeing of the labour market which made employment less secure, and the development of whole areas suffering poverty which impacted mainly on families with children. In the Czech Republic the percentage of all households with the lowest incomes was 20 per cent but this figure rose to 51 per cent for couples with three or more children (Ferge, 2000, p277). Ferge also noted that for the Czech Republic and other Central European states the figures were not entirely reliable as the Roma population was often missing from the analysis.

- Unemployment, which was virtually unknown before 1989, increased substantially from 2 to 4 per cent in 1992, 4.3 per cent in 1996, 5.8 per cent in

Jan 1998 to 6.4 per cent in Aug 1998.

- There also appeared to be an increase in crime. In 1989, 71,069 crimes were committed, while in 1995, 114,791 crimes were committed. An analysis of this phenomenon argued that *criminological investigations indicate an increase in brutality of all types of criminal activity among children and teenagers* (Chytil, 1998, p49).

Social work in the Czech Republic is delivered through a diversity of providers at the state, regional and municipal levels and through church and other non-governmental organisations (NGOs). Most services are provided by NGOs and church organisations such as the Silesians, Caritas, Diakony. Chytil suggests that there was basically no change in social work after 1989. Social workers continued to work with the same client groups and *the majority of social workers were employed by the municipal councils and as state employees at district offices* (1998, p50). Social work was still primarily based on the medical model (Monk and Singleton, 1995; Chytil,1998), psycho-educational models (Krakesova, 1973, in Chytil) and on the client as consumer (Johnson, 1998). There is some evidence that social work developments have been influenced by social work practice in the UK, particularly in so far as they have relatively early in their social work development adopted quality-assurance processes which mirror UK developments. There was an attempt to regularise social work services at end of the 1990s with the relocation of decision-making to localities. It was believed that the focus on quality assurance would *show organisations are efficient; if they are they will get accreditation and be entitled to long-term financial support. The quality standards have been developed by the Ministry of Work and Social Matters along with the DoH in the UK* (lecture by Head of Jabok College, Charles University, Prague, 2003).

The legal structure governing the delivery of social work has been in a process of evolution. The 1998 Amendment to Law Concerning Families no.91/1998 defined the rights of children to *healthy development, proper upbringing and education and the protection of their justified interests* (Pridhova, 1999, p44). Recently there have been proposals for a new law about social services to *set conditions for provision of assistance to persons in adverse social situations through the social services* (Jandejsek, 2004).

Work with the Roma

It is within this developing framework that social work intervention with the Roma can be gauged. The mobility of the Roma had been restricted by the Communist regime prior to 1989. The development of the new state did not necessarily address this problem. As Bancroft has noted, *in Central and Eastern Europe Roma are often simply being excluded from civil society altogether . . . the Czech citizenship law of 1993 . . . excluded many Czech Roma from citizenship, pushing many further to the margins of society* (Bancroft, 2005, p155). Official statistics suggested that there were 11,000–12,000 Roma in the Czech Republic. However, it is now accepted that the real figure is closer to between 200,000 and 300,000. The Roma do not constitute a homogenous group but are made up of a number of different ethnic groupings, including Slovakian Roma (largest group), Hungarian, Moravian and Sinti Roma (only a couple of hundred). While the largest population concentrations are in Prague, many live outside Prague in smaller cities such as Brno, Ostrava and Teplicsci (Office of the Government of the Czech Republic, 2003). Some key characteristics of the Roma experience are as follows.

- It is often forgotten that the Roma were the focus of an attempted genocide by the Nazis during the 1930s/1940s. It became known as the Roma Holocaust in which very significant numbers died, and is remembered every April.

- Education – a disproportionate number of Roma children attend special schools.

- Housing – Roma often live in the worst housing.

- Unemployment – there are much higher levels of unemployment among the Roma than in the general population, reaching 80–90 per cent in some areas.

In an effort to improve the social circumstances of the Roma, the Czech Republic introduced the Roma Integration Project in 2003. This sought to bring the Roma into decision-making bodies and led to the establishment of the Council for National Minorities and the Council for the Roma Minority in Prague (through which 12 deputies and 12 Roma representatives meet every two months in the Parliament building; Government of the Czech Republic, 2003).

Social exclusion remains the key experience of the Roma. This is recognised within the integration policy which suggests that integration means:

> *the full incorporation of the Roma into society while preserving most of the cultural features and differences that characterise them and that they want to preserve* provided that these differences are not against the laws of the Czech Republic Government of the Czech Republic.
>
> (Government of the Czech Republic, March 2003; emphasis added)

This led among other things to the appointment of specialist advisers, particularly at ministry, regional and district levels, the implementation of anti-discrimination measures, and affirmative action at all levels, particularly in education. However, there remain substantial problems, including;

- a lack of awareness of cultural difference;
- insufficient knowledge of Roma language and culture;
- the problem of special schools;
- inadequate social and health care.

The integration policy acknowledges this when it says that:

> *Compared to the majority of society, the Roma community is far more exposed to all the danger factors quoted by the European Social Programme, e.g. long-term unemployment, long-term low or inadequate incomes, low level of education and qualification, early school-leaving, disability, ill-health, unsatisfactory housing, sex inequality, discrimination, racism, family break-up, living in greatly disadvantaged localities, alcohol and drug addiction.*
>
> (Government of the Czech Republic, 2003, p25)

A recent report to the United Nations Human Rights Committee by The European Roma Rights Centre, Vzajemme Souziti, the Peacework Development Fund and the Centre on Housing Rights and Evictions in Europe suggested that, if anything, the discrimination against the Roma had worsened over the last few years. Anti-discriminatory legislation such as the Roma Integration Policy was not working, segregation in schools was still a major problem, Roma continued to find it difficult to access the labour market and racism was prevalent. The report argued that:

> *Regular and systematic human rights abuse of Roma in the Czech Republic is aggravated by the fact that anti-Romani hate speech is a regular part of public discourse ... Anti-Romani statements are a standard and often unquestioned part of public life in the Czech Republic.*

(European Roma Rights Centre, Vzajemme Souziti, Peacework Development Fund and the Centre on Housing Rights and Evictions in Europe, 2006).

RESEARCH SUMMARY

Reviewing the experience of Roma children in the education system, the European Roma Rights Centre said in 1999 that the:

> *disproportionate allocation to schools for the mentally handicapped affects the current and future prospects of at least 25,000 Romani children presently in primary schools in the Czech Republic, as well as numerous other Roma whose lives have been ruined by the school system ... it is clear that many educators in practice regard remedial schools as schools for Roma.*
>
> (ERRC, 1999, Section 3:1)

They add:

> *Numerous Romani parents with their children in basic schools reported to the ERRC that schooling authorities had tried to pressure them into placing their children in special schools ... no Romani parents ... had been told in detail the consequences of putting their child into remedial schools ... none had been told that following an education in a remedial/special school their children would have almost no chance of lucrative employment.*
>
> (Section 4:1)

They conclude:

> *Often Roma are blamed for their situation. Blame is often formulated as 'linguistic handicap' or 'sociocultural disadvantage', a rhetorical device which generalises the discrimination faced by Roma away from them by portraying them as somehow inevitably located on the lower margins of an otherwise dynamic society. This permits the most insidious presentations of the school as a missionary outpost for Czech civilisation, desperately trying to save children from their barbarian families.*
>
> (Section 12)

However, some of these developments are now being undermined. The move toward decentralisation has allowed each municipality to decide its own attitude toward implementing the integration policy. This has resulted in inconsistency and lack of coverage across Czech municipalities. Local authorities are not bound by the Roma Integration Policy and so they can decide not to implement it. For example, the Mayor of Teplicsci has abolished the system of Roma deputies previously in place.

What is the European Roma Rights Centre?

The European Roma Rights Centre (ERRC) is an international public interest law organisation engaging in a range of activities aimed at combating anti-Romani racism and human rights abuse of Roma. The approach of the ERRC involves, in particular, strategic litigation, international advocacy, research and policy development, and human rights training of Romani activists. Since its establishment in 1996, the ERRC has endeavoured to give Roma the tools necessary to combat discrimination and win equal access to government, education, employment, health care, housing and public services. The ERRC works to combat prejudice and discrimination against Roma, and to promote genuine equality of treatment and equality of respect.

European Roma Rights Centre: www. errc.org

Local research

The research underpinning this discussion took place in Prague and Teplisci during 2005/6 and was based on over 30 interviews and group discussions with social workers and the Roma. While the results are still being evaluated, the initial outcomes include the following;

- There is a disparity between integration policy and social work professionals' views of Roma. There is some initial evidence that the professionals working with the Roma have a negative view of the potential of the Roma, which results in a pathologisation of the Roma which has striking similarities to that outlined above.

- Discrimination in the education system is still prevalent and may be getting worse. (ERRC *et al.*, 2006, p37).

- High levels of unemployment remain.

- There is a gap between policy and practice. The reality for Roma is closer to notions of assimilation than integration.

However, in a similar way to Ireland, there are also clear signs of positive developments within the Roma community. For example, the Roma have established their own non-governmental organisation (Romodrom) which seeks to represent their interests in discussion with state and regional government bodies. Roma have also established their own internet radio station, Sdruzeni Dzeno, and the Evangelicka Akademie Prague has been established which trains Roma as pedagogues. From the interviews conducted with Roma it is clear that there is a clear commitment of individual Roma to change their and their families' circumstances. It appears that links with other Roma, through ERRC, will empower Roma internationally and a new indigenous leadership is growing, similar to the Travellers' movement in Ireland. (See the discussion of Gramsci's notion of organic intellectuals in Chapter 3, Gramsci, 1972; and MacLaughlin's discussion of 'ethnic intelligentsia' above.)

These developments suggest that there is significant scope, even within situations where discrimination may have been institutionalised for a considerable period, for people to engage with the processes of social change we described in earlier chapters. It is important to see marginalised peoples' struggle as an anti-racist one. not just a struggle for integration. However, the lessons of the Roma in the Czech Republic suggest that as social workers we need to move beyond approaches which pathologise people to recognise the potential of even the most marginalised people to initiate change.

Denmark

Background

The social work task in Denmark differs from the British and Irish experience in that 'social ardgivers' (social advisers) carry a responsibility for 'gatekeeping' the financial needs of service users (Melhbye, 1993; Pringle, 1998). The Danish government has also, through its social development programme, put a great emphasis on prevention strategies (Ministry of Health, 1994). As a consequence, there has been a *significant reduction in the number of children being removed from home over the past few decades* (Harder, 1997; Pringle, 1998, p103). However, in those cases where a decision is made to compulsorily remove a child under the provisions of the Social Assistance Act, that decision is made by a social committee in each locality, consisting of three municipal politicians, one judge and one psychologist. This decision is only made when *the child's welfare is at risk [and where] care outside their home [in a residential home or in family care], the offer of their own flat or enrolment in a continuation school etc, can be the most appropriate solution* (Ministry of Social Affairs, 1995b, pp18–19). This contrasts sharply with the British and Irish systems, where the decision is made by the courts (Pringle, 1998). In fact, in contrast to the experience in Ireland and the Czech Republic, *it remains a guiding principle that preventative social measures in Denmark be directed towards supporting the family, in such a way as to provide optimum conditions for the child's growth and development* (Ministry of Social Affairs, 1995a, p66).

Fridberg (1998) argues that in Denmark, *during the last 10 years children's issues have gradually become more visible in public discussions and a policy field of children's affairs is emerging* (p28). He concludes that the economic status of families with children is satisfactory, while acknowledging that they have on average a lower per capita income than families without children. He suggests that the *worries in Denmark are not so much about children in poor families as about children in families who for some reason are not able to take reasonable care of their children, such as children in families affected by drug or alcohol abuse* (Fridberg, 1998, p31). The Consolidation Act on Social Services 2004 continues to reflect this focus on prevention. The aims of the act are expressed as being to *offer general services designed to serve as preventative measures* and the object of the Act is *to improve the capacity of the individual recipient to be self-reliant, or to facilitate his/her daily life and enhance the quality of life* (Consolidation Act, 2004).

While the Danish welfare state is relatively generous by the standards of the rest of Europe, there are still significant problems for minority communities who may not have become integrated into Danish society. This is particularly noticeable with young people who have become alienated from the school, welfare and social protection systems.

Octopussy (Blaeksprutten, Avidovre, Copenhagen)

Octopussy is a project based in a flat in Avidovre, part of Hvidovre commune in Copenhagen. The area has one of the largest concentrations of ethnic minorities in Copenhagen, estimated to be between 30 per cent and 40 per cent of the local population. The area is one of social housing which provides accommodation for approximately 5,600 people. Octopussy is part of the SSP initiative (school, social services, police) which seeks to provide services for young people, who are disadvantaged and/or socially excluded. It works with a large number of ethnic minority young people the majority of whom are Turkish or Pakistani in origin, although there are children attending the project from Germany and from other Scandinavian countries. The aim of the project is to provide a safe environment for young people, to recognise the various reasons they may not be currently attending local schools and to seek to gain their reintegration into school. The project is headed by a Kurdish social pedagogue, the first non-Danish social pedagogue to qualify in Denmark. It employs five or six staff including social pedagogues, a teacher and a social adviser.

It organises its work with the young people by concentrating resources on the most at risk children, who are divided into A and B grades. The A group are the group with the greatest social needs and the most intensive work is done with them. They are provided with resources to improve their integration to Danish society. The B group have a more tangential relationship to the project, using it as a drop-in centre.

We have chosen to discuss the work of Octopussy because it continues to have an anti-racist agenda, although it does not specifically work with Gypsies or Roma, who are relatively rare in Scandinavia. The research involved interviewing five members of staff: four pedagogues and one teacher. At the time of our research one of the pedagogues was untrained but was due to undertake training soon. The others had qualified some time previously. The teacher had only been with the project since the end of the previous year. In addition I interviewed four young people. It was clear during my interviews with the workers in the project that they were acutely aware of issues of racism. They described the experiences many of the young people had had in other parts of Copenhagen. The most obvious and systematic elements of racism were less present in the immediate surroundings as it was very much a multi-cultural area where there appears to be a great degree of tolerance between the different groups living there. However, they were acutely aware that the young people they worked with would often have very acute experiences of racism which brought them into contact with the criminal justice system as well as schools and social services. The project leader was particularly committed to the notion of combating racism in the local area. He was aware from his own experiences of the difficulties non-Danish people could experience. He was currently trying to influence the education of ped-agogues and social advisers so that racism became a much more integral part of the training curriculum.

All the young people interviewed recounted instances of racism which they had experienced on a fairly regular basis. They also made the point that they did not experience racism within Octopussy itself or even within the geographical area in which Octopussy was based. However, it was a major problem in other parts of Copenhagen and they spoke of their concern about the activities of the Green Jackets, a neo-Nazi group of young people who had adopted skinhead motifs and who pro-moted the idea of Denmark being for Danes.

Clearly the project adopts an explicit anti-racist perspective in the work in which it engages. Its methodology combines both casework and groupwork approaches and is clearly predicated on the need to enhance the self-esteem and self-confidence of the young people using the project. It also recognises the need to tackle the broader causes of social exclusion. The workers involved are seeking to influence the training of social professionals within Denmark and they are also involved through their union in promoting a commitment to anti-racism in Denmark.

The project leader points out that this is not always easy. Describing the experience of the young people he works with, he says:

> We want to create a more stable life, give them more security, let them know that they may have trouble in their situation, but they have control of themselves and can be masters of their situation. From my own experience, and my family''s experience, I have not experienced racism but the stories in the media make me think. I think the ethnic minorities and social society need to enter dialogue. They both need to know about each other. This may not take all the discrimination away but it may minimise it.

One of his colleagues saw this as a major challenge for Danish pedagogy. He said that *when we treat them [the young people] as individuals we want to make them strong, to be able to stand up and say, Yes, I am Turkish, I have my identity. I am Turkish and I am able to fight as a Turk and I am strong in my person and am able to stand up for that when I go out* (interviews in Denmark 1998–2000).

One of the project leaders at Blaeksprutten describes the difficulties people often face when they try to explain the nature of their difficulties to people in agencies, including social care agencies:

A woman is living with a man in a family together, he is violent towards her. Whenever it happens she goes to some social assistants who really pity her. They say 'I feel really sorry for you'. She says that is not what she needs. She needs someone to cry out and say 'do something about it. Rise up and do something yourself.' The system does not really handle the problem, we do not really involve ourselves, we just listen.

Another project leader of a different community project points to the need for agencies to work with both excluded and mainstream people. He suggests that:

There are many voluntary institutions working with people to take care of them, but there are no resources to take them on. That is what's special about us. We try to work with the excluded and the majority. We feel that if you want to integrate people in society you have to work with all groups.

ACTIVITY 7.3

Taking one of the above countries as an example, map the social work activity described against the National Occupational Standards for either social or community work (see Chapter 3). Outline three ways in which the NOS outlined at the beginning of this chapter could be met by the type of intervention described. Evaluate how that might contribute to a change of focus within your own training.

Comment

You may wish to look at the web addresses below to gain a further insight into the issues discussed.

The above examples illustrate a diversity of practice but a common thread. They are predicated on the belief that even those people facing the most extreme forms of marginalisation and exclusion have the capacity to engage with processes of social change. They provide an important model of the forms of practice outlined in Chapters 2 and 3 and a way of establishing the legitimacy of social work and community work practice.

C H A P T E R   S U M M A R Y

This chapter has sought to take forward the discussion in Chapter 6 of international approaches to social work, particularly pedagogy. It attempts to show how social work across Europe, while sharing common concerns, is often a product of the particular national context within which it develops. It shows how the managerial discourses which have had such a significant impact on UK social work, while providing challenges to social work in other countries, are not so embedded in day-to-day practice.

The chapter then looked at the experience of an innovative range of projects in Ireland, the Czech Republic and Denmark. The Irish project, the Traveller Visibility Group, seeks to promote the empowerment of Irish Travellers and to challenge negative media projections of Travellers. The Czech discussion highlights the way in which the Roma in the Czech Republic are reacting against the discrimination they face and developing their own analysis of their situation. Both examples highlight the potential for radical social and community action highlighted in

Chapters 2 and 3 and demonstrate the way in which people facing significant marginalisation and disadvantage can develop their own indigenous leadership, what MacLauglin has called an 'ethnic intelligentsia' and Gramsci described as 'organic intellectuals'. They can also be seen to demonstrate the way European traditions of social work can have relevance to current UK practice both in terms of the radical agenda and in the way they develop interactions with the people with whom they work – the pedagogy agenda.

The chapter concluded with a discussion of a project for disaffected young people in Denmark, Blaeksprutten or Octopussy, which seeks to reintegrate them into society. It demonstrates how the pedagogic principles outlined in Chapter 6 are implemented in practice.

WEBSITES

Ireland
Combat Poverty Agency	**www.cpa.ie**
Irish Traveller Movement	**www.itmtrav.com/publications**
National Consultative Committee on Racism and Interculturalism	**www.nccri.ie**

Czech Republic
Roma in the Czech Republic	**www.romove.radio.cz/en**
Sdruzenu Dzeno	**www.dzeno.cz**
Romodrom	**www.romodrom.org**

Denmark
Ministry of Social Affairs and Ministry of Gender Equality	**www.denmark.dk/portal/page**
Consolidation Act on Social Services 2004	**www.eng.social.dk/index**
Centre for Alternative Social Analysis	**www.casa-analyse.dk**

Other
Centre for the Study of Poverty and Social Justice	**www.bristol.ac.uk/sps/research/cpsi**
Information for Practice	**www.nyu.edu/socialwork/ip**
European Roma Rights Centre	**www.errc.org**

Chapter 8

Conclusion: New parameters for social work?

The preceding chapters have sought to outline some of the challenges and opportunities facing social work today. We have looked at how issues of inclusion, inter-professionalism and internationalism have moved toward the top of social work's agenda. Yet these debates have themselves been shown to be problematic. *Inclusion*, while a key emphasis in virtually all new policy and legal developments in social work/social care/health and education, is a contested concept. Many people using services have raised issues about the adequacy of the frameworks developed to implement this inclusion agenda. They point to the way that inclusion is often framed as an agenda item by those who control the social work agenda. They ask, how real is this involvement? What resources are available to support inclusion processes? What processes of evaluation and accountability have been built in to ensure that inclusion is properly participatory and, perhaps, more importantly, how can people using services and their carers gain control of the resources and services to fully ensure that their needs are met?

These questions are particularly pertinent given the other key policy agenda which is to ensure the joined-up nature of services, most commonly through notions of *partnership, collaboration and inter-professional working*. While the Climbié Inquiry, the Clunis inquiry and the other reports which have identified gaps in existing provision point to the need for greater cooperation and understanding between services, this must not be at the expense of the participation and partnership arrangements we are developing with service users and carers. A clear danger of this increased inter-professional activity could be the further erosion of the power of the user of services. As we have indicated earlier, inclusion and inter-professionalism, without an acknowledgement of power differentials, are a mere tokenistic response to the problems we identify.

The themes we identified in the Introduction are now becoming clearer. They cross-cut with each other to give us the beginnings of a framework for understanding how social work may develop in the future. In earlier chapters we have examined the way debates around inclusion, inter-professionalism and internationalism are key to the future direction of social work. The drive behind these initiatives may well come from discourses within the current social policy agenda and the attempt to regulate social work in such a way that its aim to achieve meaningful social change is marginalised. This is particularly true within a philosophy which promotes the acquisition of knowledge and skills within a competency framework driven by the Quality Assurance Agency and the National Occupational Standards. However, the same frameworks, if interpreted within a discourse which seeks to empower users and carers within social work services, provides an opportunity to promote the social change perspective which has been critical to the development of social work since its inception (Kendall, 2001; also see Chapters 2 and 3).

The inter-cutting themes of the book can now be seen to converge. We noted in Chapter 5 the way different policy developments have promoted the idea of participation and inclusion, yet have done so in a way which is not always measurable. They may in fact not only appear to be tokenistic, but if placed within an analytical framework which seeks to evaluate service user/care involvement may actually be shown to be so.

In turn, debates around professionalism cannot be separated from debates around inter-professionalism. If the development of our professional identity is itself predicated on the development of processes of exclusion and ways of protecting ourselves *vis-à vis* other emergent and established professionals (precisely the process we have argued against in the development of our own professional identity), how much more powerful are these processes when we link with other professionals?

The final part of the equation occurs when we talk about partnership. Clearly this is not the same as inter-professionalism in that it suggests equality between partners and may occur at a range of levels – between agencies, agencies and service users/ carers, across networks, etc. However it occurs, how much can this notion of partnership be enhanced if we begin to engage with social workers in other countries, from whose traditions we can learn and with whom we can share elements of our best practice?

These potential points of connection can provide a possible framework for a new form of social work practice. The remainder of this chapter seeks to map out the way this may occur. Figure 8.1 (opposite) illustrates how these processes occur and how they intersect with each other. The diagonal boxes show the interrelationships of the key factors; for example, the downward-facing triangle shows the relationship between the key themes in current social work of inter-professionalism and internationalism and that, if they are to be effective they need to be underpinned by processes of inclusion. Instead of enhancing the power of social workers by making their decision-making even more remote from the experience of people who use social work services, they are then grounded in the day-to-day reality of service users and carers. Such an inversion of the 'normal' relationships in social work helps ensure its relevance to current societal developments.

The upward-facing triangle reflects the underpinning issues which help achieve this goal. Partnership is integral to developing models of inclusion. Properly understood, it does not mean the enhancement of the effectiveness of the professional but has more to do with creating conditions of equality so that each partner's contribution is regarded as of equal value. Participation suggests that this process of partnership is active and is based on engagement and the empowerment of all people using social work services. This does not necessarily mean rejecting current moves to professionalise social work but it does mean developing new concepts of professionalism grounded in participation and partnership. It therefore suggests a model of professional practice which is reflexive, responsive and open and which does not use professionalism as a way to exclude either other professionals or service users and

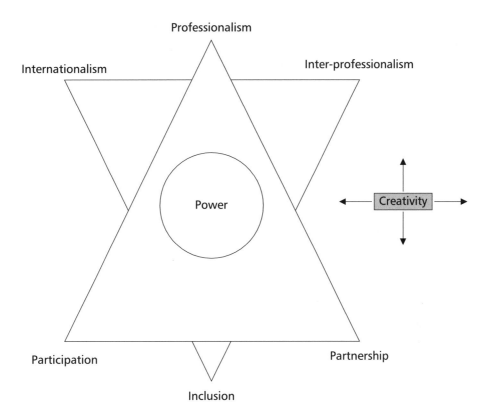

Figure 8.1 The new framework for social work?

carers. This suggests that it is possible to develop a model of professional practice which while conscious of the need to ensure standards of good practice is also accountable, not just to other social workers but also to those who use social work services.

These two sets of relationships – *internationalism, inter-professionalism and inclusion* and *professionalism, participation and partnership* – are based on a conception of power which is multi-faceted and which not only seeks to understand how power works on social workers and those who use services but also how power can be used to challenge inequality and disadvantage and promote more equitable social relationships. A central element in any newly configured social work is then about both recognising the power we have and wherever possible seeking to share it with the people with whom we work. A key task for social work is therefore the creation of an empowered and active group of service users and carers who hold us to account, share in our decision-making and participate actively in the way we deliver our services.

The earlier chapters have provided some indications of how these processes can occur. Chapter 1 looked at models of policy analysis and asked how they reflected contemporary social work. Superficially the pluralist view seemed to suggest that power could be gained by well-organised groups while the structuralist argument appears to foreclose action to redress inequality because of the powerful interests currently wielding power and the unlikelihood of them relinquishing it. The book has sought to demonstrate that neither model provides a full account of the way we can achieve change as social workers. Indeed, the benefit of current developments around choice, control and independence may well be that we no longer see the acquisition of power as beyond our abilities or aspirations but as something attainable through the promotion of our own self activity and that of the people we work with.

Chapters 2 and 3 took this analysis forward, arguing that social work has a rich tradition on which it should draw to revitalise its practice. Radical social and community work demonstrate how a focus on wider social structures can complement work at the individual level. Chapter 3 in particular shows how the core values of social work and community work share a common concern with tackling discrimination and promoting empowerment.

As a social work educator, the author is often told by qualifying and post-qualifying students that it is not possible to practise in any way other than through an instrumental and managerialist perspective within the statutory sector. Leaving aside the argument that this suggests a degree of control over social work by agencies of which even the Stasi would have been proud, it also denies the possibility that social workers can themselves be active change agents. It is almost as if empowerment is something which happens to others but not something to which we can aspire. Hopefully the lesson of this book is that it is possible to negotiate space to achieve such change. Indeed, Foucault has suggested that *all of my investigations rest on a postulate of absolute optimism* (Foucault, 1991, p174). He added that *the problems I pose are always concerned with local and particular issues* (p150). By analysing power, he suggests, *those who are inserted in certain relations of power, who are implicated in them, might escape them through their actions of resistance and rebellion, might transform them in order not to be subjugated any longer* (p174).

A useful counterpoint to this conservatism in some UK practice is provided by an example from the international arena. Rowe *et al.* (2000) interviewed 45 social workers from throughout the world, affiliated to the International Federation of Social Workers (IFSW). They found that for *the majority of respondents and especially for those practising in developing countries, participation and empowerment were essential components of social and community development* (p68). Their respondents mention women's rights, HIV/Aids, child welfare, community development, disability and environmental degradation as issues with which it was possible to transcend national borders and develop new forms of practice.

Chapter 4 showed how these pressures towards a more conservative form of practice are not peculiar to statutory social work but are also present in the voluntary or third sector. It seeks to show that agencies can resist these constraints and develop ways of working which are enabling and empowering.

Chapter 5 looked at how one response to these issues was gaining prominence. The involvement of service users and carers in social work is now at the core of all recent policy and legislative developments. This can present another set of problems – how can we be sure that any involvement that is developed is real and not merely tokenistic? The chapter suggested a model of participation and inclusion which placed service users and carers in control of the interventions with which they engaged. Chapters 6 and 7 then sought to suggest the importance of looking outside the UK for models with which we could take forward our own practices. These chapters argued that this is a reciprocal process but that we can learn a great deal from engaging with ideas from elsewhere. In particular, recent work by the Thomas Coram Research Unit, supported by the DfES and DoH, looking at the relevance of social pedagogy to work with children and young people, provides an exciting opportunity to consider ways in which our own practice can be revitalised.

Finally, we need to consider how we can make our practice more relevant to the concerns of people who use services. The discussion of the 'common third' in Chapter 6 suggests a means of doing this. The common third is based on the idea of social workers/pedagogues coming to situations as partners and creating, through music, drama, etc., a joint activity in which neither is the expert and in which each makes an equal contribution. The purpose is to develop the self-esteem and self-confidence of the person using the service so that they can take that new self-belief forward into other areas of their lives and become fully empowered citizens. Central to this approach is the notion of creativity which we alluded to in the introduction and to which we have returned at various stages in the text. The reintroduction of creativity into both the academic curricula and practice environment is an important means of taking social work forward and reclaiming the traditions which placed both person-centred, humanistic practice and social change at the top of the social work agenda. The model therefore places creativity as a core activity in the new social work framework.

The book concluded with a discussion of the way social work in other countries, in particular Ireland, the Czech Republic and Denmark, provides useful examples of a more engaged form of practice in which service users not only develop their own organisations but form their own leadership and challenge traditional relationships between professionals and people using services. Their example indicates that the way we relate to people using services is in its infancy and that only when we begin to cede control of services to those using them will we be able to claim that we now have real, accountable and person-centred social and community services.

Creative Social Work at the University of Portsmouth
- Create a group of service users/carers, students and staff from the Centre for Social work and the School of Creative and Performing Arts.
- Creative workshop – January 2007 – produced in partnership with Social Work Inclusion Group, students (UK and international) and academic staff.
- Curriculum – at undergraduate level the exploration of issues of identity, difference and discrimination through creative activity, at postgraduate level the development of two units where the assessment is based on the production of creative artefacts such as performance, music, creative writing, poetry, etc.

Two short excerpts from the work of the Creative Writing Group at Portsmouth illustrate the core themes of the book.

See us as people, not just as a case
Others are just as important
Come, learn what we have to say
I am the expert on my case
Authority and power should come from us
Listen!

Work with us
Our experiences are very valuable
Respect goes both ways
Knowledge is not just academic

(Creative Writing Working Party, Summer 2006)

Method

Take one Social Services Department.
Add a good SWIG of service users and carers and a promising mix of students.
Mix well and brew slowly for three years.
Leave open for experience.

(Creative Writing Working Party, Summer 2006)

References

Aabro, C (2004) *The common third*. Written correspondence with author.

Abbott, P and Wallace, C (1990) *An introduction to sociology; feminist perspectives*. London: Routledge.

Abrahamson, P (1997) Combating poverty and social exclusion in Europe. In Beck, W, van der Maesen, L and Walker, A (eds) *The social quality of Europe*. Bristol: The Policy Press.

Ackerson, BJ and Harrison, D (2000) Practitioners' perceptions of empowerment. *Families in Society: The Journal of Contemporary Human Services*, 81 (3), 238–45.

Adams, R (1996) – *Social work and empowerment*. Basingstoke: Macmillan.

Adams, R, Dominelli, L and Payne, M (2005) *Social work futures: crossing boundaries, transforming practice*. Basingstoke: Palgrave/Macmillan.

Ahmad, B (1990) *Black perspectives in social work*. Birmingham: Venture Press.

Alinsky, S (1971) *Rules for radicals*. New York: Random House.

Allman, P (2001) *Revolutionary social transformation: democratic hopes, political possibilities and critical education*. Westport, CT: Bergin and Garvey.

Aluffi-Pentini, A and Lorenz, W (1996) *Anti-racist work with young people: European experiences and approaches*. Lyme Regis: Russell House.

Arnstein, S (1969) A ladder of citizen participation. *Journal of the American Institute of Planners,* 35 (4), 214–24.

Aspis, S (1997) Self-advocacy for people with learning difficulties; does it have a future?, *Disability and Society*, 12 (4), 647–54.

Aspis, S (2002) Self-advocacy: vested interests and misunderstandings, *British Journal of Learning Disabilities*, 30, 3–7.

ATD Fourth World (2005) *Getting the right trainers – enabling service users to train social work students and practitioners about the reality of family poverty in the UK*. London: ATD Fourth World.

Avramov, D (1997) Homelessness in the European Union: changes and continuities. In Avramov, D (ed.) *Youth homelessness in the european union*. Belgium: FEANTSA.

Bailey, R and Brake, M (1980) Contributions to a radical practice in social work. In Brake, M and Bailey, R (eds) *Radical social work and practice*. London: Edward Arnold.

Bailey, R and Brake, M (eds) (1975) *Radical social work*. London: Edward Arnold.

Baistow, K (1994) Liberation and regulation? Some paradoxes of empowerment, *Critical Social Policy*, 14 (3), 34–46.

Barry, M (1998) Social exclusion and social work: an introduction. In Barry, M and Hallett C (eds) *Social exclusion and social work: issues of theory, policy and practice*. Lyme Regis: Russell House.

Barry, M and Hallett C (eds) (1998) *Social exclusion and social work: issues of theory, policy and practice*. Lyme Regis: Russell House.

Bateman, N (2006) *Practising welfare rights*. London: Routledge/Community Care.

Bauman, Z (2001) *Community – seeking safety in an insecure world*. Cambridge: Polity Press.

Bennett, F and Roberts M (2004) *From input to influence – participatory approaches to research and inquiry into poverty*. York: Joseph Rowntree Foundation.

Benwell Community Development Project (1974) *Final report*. London: HMSO.

Beresford, P (1996) Challenging the 'them' and 'us' of social policy research. In Dean, H (ed.) Ethics and social policy research. Bedfordshire: University of Luton Press/Social Policy Association.

Beresford P and Campbell, J (1994) Disabled people, service users, user Involvement and representation, *Disability and Society*, 9 (3), 315–24.

Beresford, P and Croft, S (1993) *Citizen Involvement: a practical guide*. Basingstoke: Macmillan.

Beresford, P and Croft, S (1995) It's our problem too: challenging the exclusion of poor people from poverty discourse, *Critical Social Policy*, 44/45.

Beresford, P and Holden, C (2000) We have choices: globalisation and welfare user movements, *Disability and Society*, 15 (7) 973–89.

Beresford, P and Hoban, M (2005) *Participation in anti-poverty and regeneration work and research: Overcoming barriers and creating opportunities*. York: Joseph Rowntree Foundation.

Beresford, P and Turner, M (1997) *It's our welfare: report of the citizen's commission on the future of the welfare state*. London: National Institute of Social Work.

Beresford, P, Green, D, Lister, R and Woodward, K (1999) *Poverty first hand: poor people speak for themselves*. London: Child Poverty Action Group.

Berry, L, Cannan, C and Lyons, K (1992) *Social work in Europe*. Basingstoke: Macmillan.

Boddy, J, Cameron, C, Hepinstall, McQuail, S and Petrie, P (2003) *Working with children: social pedagogy and residential child care in Europe (draft report)*. London: Department of Health.

Boddy, J, Cameron, C, Moss, P, Mooney, A, Petrie, P and Statham, J (2005) *Introducing pedagogy into the children's workforce: Children's workforce strategy: a response to the consultation document*. London: Thomas Coram Research Unit.

Bolger, S, Corrigan, P, Docking, J and Frost, N (1981) *Towards socialist welfare work*. Basingstoke: Macmillan.

Borghill, L (2004) *The empowerment of young people at risk through sport and outdoor activities*. Unpublished undergraduate dissertation, Portsmouth University.

Bown, K (2004) *Involving young people in research – some reflections*. Paper presented to PIMHS Research Group, University of Portsmouth.

Boylan, J and Ing, P (2005) 'Seen but not heard' – young people's experience of advocacy, *International Journal of Social Welfare*, 14, 2–12.

Brah, A (1992) Difference, diversity and differentiation. In Donald, J and Rattansi, A (eds) *'Race', culture and difference*. London: SAGE/Open University Press.

Brake, M and Bailey, R (eds) (1980) *Radical social work and practice*. London: Edward Arnold.

Braye, S (2000) Participation and involvement in social care. In Kemshall, H and Littlechild, R (eds) *User involvement and participation in social care: research informing practice*. London: Jessica Kingsley.

Brueggemann, WG (2006) *The practice of macro social work*. 3rd edition. Belmont, CA: Thomson Brooks/Cole.

Buckley, H, Skehill, C and O'Sullivan, E (1997) *Child protection practices in Ireland: a case study*. Dublin: Oak Tree Press.

Burns, D Hambleton, R and Hoggett, P (1994) *The politics of decentralisation: revitalising local democracy*. Basingstoke: Macmillan.

Byrne, D (1999) *Social exclusion*. Buckingham: Open University Press.

Cabinet Office and HM Treasury (2006) *The future role of the third sector in social and economic regeneration: interim report*. London, HMSO.

Cameron, C (2004) Social pedagogy and care: Danish and German practice in young people's residential care, *Journal of Social Work*, 4 (2), 133–51.

Cameron C, McQuail, S and Petrie, P (2007*) Implementing the social pedagogic approach for workforce training and education in England: a preliminary study*. London: Thomas Coram Research Unit, University of London/Cabinet Office/Department for Education and Skills.

Campbell, J and McColgan, M (2002) Social work in Northern Ireland. In Payne, M and Shardlow, S *Social work in the British Isle*s. London: Jessicca Kingsley.

Campbell, J and Oliver, M (1996) *Disability politics: understanding our past, changing our future*. Basingstoke: Macmillan.

Carr, S (2004) *Has service user participation made a difference to social care services?* London: Social Care Institute of Excellence, Position Paper No 3.

Cassell, P (1993) *The Giddens Reader*. Basingstoke: Macmillan.

Cassidy, L and Jakes, S (undated) Evaluating the national outcomes: programme outcomes for communities, citizen development. Downloaded from **http://ag.arizona. edu/fcs/cyfernet/nowg/ cd-litrev.html, 17/10/05.**

Centre for Enterprise and Economic Development Research (CEEDR) (2001) *Final report to the Small Business Service*. London: Middlesex University Business School.

Chambers, H (2004) *Creative arts and play for the well-being of looked after children*. Highlight no. 212. London: National Children's Bureau.

Charity Commission (2007) *Stand and deliver: the future for charities delivering public services*. Liverpool: Charity Commission Publications.

Children's Rights Alliance and National Youth Council of Ireland (2002) *Hearing young voices*. Dublin: downloaded from **www.youth.ie/research/execut.html** on 17/10/05.

Chouan, K, Esmail, U, Joseph, J, Mathal, K and Modayil, J (1996) Anti-racism and black empowerment in Britain: principles and case studies. In Aluffi-Pentini, A and Lorenz, W (eds) *Anti-racist work with young people: European experiences and approaches*. Lyme Regis: Russell House.

Chytil, O (1998) Social work in the Czech Republic, *Social Work in Europe*, 5 (3), 48–55.

Chytil, O and Popelkova, R (2000) Social policy and social work in the Czech Republic. In Adams, A Erath, P and Shardlow, S *Key themes in European social work: theory, practice, perspectives*. Lyme Regis: Russell House.

Clarke, J, Langan, M and Williams, F (2001) Remaking welfare: the British welfare regime in the 1980s and 1990s. In Cochrane, A, Clarke J and Gewirtz, S *Comparing welfare states*. (2nd edition). London SAGE/Open University Press.

Commission for Social Care Inspection (2005) *Making every child matter*. Newcastle: Office of the Children's Rights Inspector.

Commission for Social Care Inspection (2006a) *Real voices, real choices*. Newcastle: Office of the Children's Rights Inspector.

Commission for Social Care Inspection (2006b) *Young people's views on leaving care*. Newcastle: Office of the Children's Rights Inspector.

Commission for Social Care Inspection (2007) *Care Matters: Children's views on the government Green Paper*. Newcastle, Office of the Children's Rights Inspector.

Community Development Projects (1974) *Inter-project report*. London: HMSO.

Community Development Projects (1977) *Gilding the ghetto*. London: HMSO.

Consolidation Act on Social Services (2004) Ministry of Social Affairs, Copenhagen, Denmark.

Corkey, D and Craig, C (1978) CDP: community work and class politics. In Corno, P (ed.) *Political issues in community work*. London: Routledge & Kegan Paul.

Cornwell, N (1994) Social work education and practice sans frontiers, *Issues in Social Work Education*, 14,1.

Corrigan, P and Leonard, P (1978) *Social work under capitalism*. Basingstoke: Macmillan.

Council of Europe (2004) *Final report of the activity carried out in 2003–2004.* European Committee for Social Cohesion (CDCS), Group of specialists on User Involvement in Social Services and Integrated Social Services Delivery (CS-US). Strasbourg: Council of Europe.

Craig, C, Gorman, M and Vercseg, I (2004) The Budapest Declaration: building civil society through community development, *Community Development Journal*, 39 (40), 423–9.

Craig, C, Taylor, M and Parker, T (2004) Protest or partnership? The voluntary and community sectors in the policy process, *Social Policy and Administration*, 38 (3), 221–31.

Creative Writing Working Party (2006) *Poems from the creative writing working party*. Portsmouth: University of Portsmouth.

Croft, S and Beresford, P (1998) Postmodernity and the future of welfare: whose critiques, whose social policy? In Carter, J (1998) *Post-modernity and the fragmentation of welfare*. London: Routledge.

Crouch, C (1999) *Social change in western Europe*. Oxford: Oxford University Press.

Dalrymple, J (2004) Developing the concept of professional advocacy: an examination of the role of child youth advocates in England and Wales, *Journal of Social Work* 4 (2), 179–97.

Darton, D and Streliz, J (2003) *Tackling poverty and disadvantage in the twenty-first century*. York: Joseph Rowntree Foundation.

Davis, A and Wainwright, S (2005) Combating poverty and social exclusion: implications for social work education, *Social Work Education*, 24 (3), 259–73.

Day, G (2006) *Community and everyday life*. London: Routledge.

DETR (Department of the Environment, Transport and the Regions) (1998) *Guidance on enhancing public participation in local government*. London: DETR.

Department of Health (1995) *Messages from research*. London: HMSO.

Department of Health (1998) *Modernising social services*. London: HMSO.

Department of Health (2001) *Valuing People: A new strategy for learning disability for the 21st century*. London: HMSO.

Department of Health (2005a) *Independence, well-being and choice*. London: HMSO.

Department of Health (2005b) – *Responses to the consultation on adult social care in England; analysis of feedback from the Green Paper, Independence, well being and choice*. London: Department of Health.

Department of Health (2006) *Our health, our care, our say*. London: HMSO.

Department for Work and Pensions (2005) *Opportunity for all: a summary of the seventh annual report*. London: HMSO.

Doel, M and Williams, C (2002) Social work in Wales. In Payne, M and Shardlow,S *Social work in the British Isles*. London: Jessicca Kingsley.

Dominelli, L (1990) *Women and community action*. Birmingham: Venture Press.

Dominelli, L (1997) *Anti-racist social work*. 2nd edition. Basingstoke: Macmillan.

Domiinelli, L (1997) *Sociology for social work*. Basingstoke: Palgrave.

Dominelli, L (1998) *Anti-oppressive practice in context*. In Adams, R, Dominelli, L and Payne, M *Social work: themes, issues and critical debates*. Basingstoke: Macmillan.

Dominelli, L (1999) Neo-liberalism, social exclusion and welfare clients in a global economy, *International Journal of Social Welfare*, 8, 14–22.

Dominelli, L (2004) *Social work: theory and practice for a changing profession*. Cambridge: Polity Press.

Dominelli, L and Hoogvelt, A (1996) Globalisation and the technocratisation of social work, *Critical Social Policy*, 47, 16 (2), 45–62.

Drake, RF (1999) *Understanding disability policies*. Basingstoke: Macmillan.

Driver, S and Martell, L (1998) – *New Labour, politics after Thatcherism*. Cambridge: Polity Press.

Dunst, CJ, Trivette, CM and Deal, A (1994) Meaning and characteristics of empowerment. In Dunst, CJ Trivette, CM and Deal (eds) *Supporting and strengthening families: methods, strategies and practices*, Cambridge, MA: Brookline Books.

Eichstellar, G and Raper, D (2006) *Treasure hunt: searching for pedagogic ideas within youth work in Portsmouth*. Paper presented to the What is a pedagogue? conference, London, Thomas Coram Research Unit.

Erath, P, Hamalainen, J and Sing, H (2000) Comparing social work from a European perspective: towards a comparative science of social work. In Adams, A, Erath, P and Shardlow, S *Key themes in European social work: theory, practice, perspectives*. Lyme Regis: Russell House.

Etzioni, A (1993) *The spirit of community*. London: Fontana Press.

European Commission (1995) *Final report on the implementation of the Community programme concerning the economic and social integration of the economically and socially less priviliged groups in society, Poverty 3 (1989–94)*. Brussels: Commission of the European Communities.

European Committee for Social Cohesion (CDCS)/Group of Specialists on user involvement in social services and integrated service delivery. Final report of the activity carried out in 2003–4, Brussels: Council of Europe (downloaded from **www.coe.int/T/E/Social_cohesion/Social_Policies/04.activities** 10/10/05.

Evers, A (2004) *Current strands in debating user involvement in social services*. Brussels: Council of Europe (downloaded from **www.coe.int/T/E/Social_cohesion/Social_Policies/04.activities** 10/10/05.

Fanon, F (1971) *The wretched of the earth*. London: Penguin.

Fanon, F (1978) *Black skin, white masks*. London: Penguin.

Feldon, P (1975) Radical soft cops destroy capitalist society by withdrawing their labour permanently. *Case Con*, 19.

Ferguson, H and Powell, F (2002) Social work in late modern Ireland. In Payne, M and Shardlow, S *Social work in the British Isles*. London: Jessicca Kingsley.

Fook, J (1999) Critical reflectivity in education and practice. In Pease, B and Fook, J (eds) *Transforming social work practice: postmodern critical perspectives*. London: Routledge.

Fook, J (2002) *Social work: critical theory and practice*. London: SAGE.

Foucault, M (1980) *Power/knowledge: Selected interviews and other writings*. Brighton: Harvester Wheatsheaf.

Foucault, M (1981) *Remarks on Marx*. New York, Semiotext (E).

Fox Harding, L (1997) *Perspectives in child care policy*. 2nd edition. Harlow: Longman.

Freeman, F, Morrison, A, Lockhart, F and Swanson, M (1996) Consulting service users: the views of young people. In Hill, M and Aldgate, J (eds) *Child welfare services: developments in law, policy, practice and research*. London: Jessica Kingsley.

Freeman,R, Chamberlayne P, Cooper, A and Rustin, M (1999) *Conclusion: A new culture of welfare*. In Chamberlayne, P Cooper, A Freeman, R and Rustin, M *Welfare and Culture in Europe: towards a new paradigm in social policy*. London: Jessica Kingsley.

Freire, P (1972) *Pedagogy of the oppressed*. London: Penguin.

Fremeaux, I (2005) New Labour's appropriation of the concept of community: a critique, *Community Development Journal,* 40 (3), 265–74.

Fridberg, T (1998) Denmark in European Observatory on National Family Policies – *Developments in family policies in 1996*. Keighley: European Commission.

Gallagher, A (1977) Women and Community Work. In Mayo, M (ed.) *Women in the Community*. London: Routledge & Kegan Paul.

Giarchi, GG and Lankshear, G (1998) The eclipse of social work in europe, *Social Work in Europe*, 5 (3), 25–36.

Giddens, A (1971) *Capitalism and modern social theory: an analysis of the writings of Marx, Durkheim and Max Weber*. Cambridge: Cambridge University Press.

Gil, DG (1998) *Confronting injustice and oppression: concepts and strategies for social workers*. New York: Columbia University Press.

Gilchrist, A (1994) *Community Work Skills Manual*, 20–21. Newcastle: Association of Community Workers.

Ginsburg, N (1992) *Divisions of welfare: a critical introduction to comparative social policy*. London: SAGE.

Glennerster, H (1999) Which welfare states are most likely to survive?, *International Journal of Social Welfare*, 8, 2–13.

Golightley, M (2006) *Social work and mental health*. 2nd edition. Exeter: Learning Matters.

Gordon, D and Townsend, P (2000) *Breadline Europe: the measurement of poverty*. Bristol: Policy Press.

Gordon, G (1980) *Michel Foucault Power/knowledge: selected interviews and other writings 1972–1977*. Brighton: Harvester Wheatsheaf.

Gould, A (1993) *Capitalist welfare systems: a comparison of Japan, Britain and Sweden.* Harlow: Longman.

Gramsci, A (1971) *Selections from the prison notebooks.* London: Lawrence and Wishart.

Groch, SA (1994) Oppositional consciousness: its manifestation and development. The case of people with disabilities, *Sociological Inquiry*, 64, 4.

Gutierrez, L (1990) Working with Women of color: an empowerment perspective, *Social Work,* 35 (2), 149–53.

Gutierrez, L, Glenmaye, L and Delois, K (1995) The organizational context of empowerment practice: implications for social work administration, *Social Work*, 40, 2.

Gutierrez, LM and Lewis, EA (1999) *Empowering women of color.* New York: Columbia University Press.

Hallerod, B and Heikkila, M (1999) Poverty and social exclusion in the Nordic countries. In Kautto, M, Heikkila, M, Hvinden, B, Marklund, S, Heikkila, M and Julkunen, I (2004) *Obstacles to an increased user involvement in social services.* Council of Europe, Brussels: Group of Specialists in Social Services (downloaded from **www.coe.int/T/E/Social_cohesion/Social_Policies/04.activities** 10/10/05).

Hamalainen, J (2003) The concept of social pedagogy in the field of social work, *Journal of Social Work*, 3 (1), 70–80.

Hanmer, J and Statham, D (1999) *Women and social work: towards women centred practice.* Basingstoke: Macmillan.

Hardcastle, DA (2004) Globalisation, welfare states and social work. In Ngoh-Tiong T and Rowlands, A *Social work around the World III*. Switzerland: International Federation of Social Workers.

Harder, M (1997) Child protection in Denmark. In Harder, M and Pringle, K *Protecting children in Europe: towards a new millenium.* Aalborg: Aalborg University Press.

Harris, A (1994) *Community work skills manual.* Newcastle: Association of Community Workers.

Hatton, K (1999) *Developing post-graduate social work training: European cooperation around curricular design and delivery.* Paper presented at the EAIE Conference, Maastricht.

Hatton, K (2001) Translating values: making sense of different value bases – reflections from Denmark and the UK, *International Journal of Social Research Methodology*, 4 (4), 265–78.

Hatton, K (2006) Europe and the undergraduate programme. In Lyons, K and Lawrence, S *Social work in Europe: educating for change.* Birmingham: BASW/Venture Press.

Hatton, K and Nugent, C (1993) *Empowerment: professionalism's achilles heel.* Paper presented to the Facing the European Challenge – the Role of the Professions in a wider Europe, Conference, Leeds University, July.

Haughey,M (1991) Confronting the pedagogical issues, *Open Learning*: November.

Hawtin, M, Hughes, G and Percy-Smith, J (1994) *Community profiling – auditing social needs.* Buckingham: Open University Press.

Hayden, C (1999) *State child care: looking after children?* London: Jessica Kingsley.

Healy, K (2000) *Social work practices: contemporary perspectives on change.* London: SAGE.

Heikkila, M and Julkunen, I (2003) *Obstacles to an increased user involvement in social services.* Strasbourg: Council of Europe.

Henderson, P and Thomas, DN (1980) *Skills in neighbourhood work.* London: National Institute for Social Work, Allen and Unwin.

Henderson, P and Glen, A (2006) From recognition to support: Community development workers in the UK, *Community Development Journal*, 41 (3), 277–92.

Hersov, J (1992) Advocacy – Issues for the 1990s. In Thompson, T and Mathias, P *Standards in mental handicap*. London: Bailliere and Tindall.

Higham, P (2001) Changing practice and an emerging social pedagogue paradigm in England: the role of the personal adviser, *Social Work in Europe,* 8 (1), 21–8.

Hill, M (2005) *The public policy process*. Harlow: Pearson/Longman.

Hindess, B (1996) *Discourses of power; from Hobbes to Foucault*. Oxford: Blackwell.

Hirschman, AO (1970) *Exit, voice and loyalty*. Cambridge, MA: Harvard University Press.

HM Government (2006) *Working together to safeguard children*. London: HMSO.

Hoggett, P (ed.) (1997) *Contested communities: experiences, struggles, policies*. Bristol: Policy Press.

Horncastle, J and Brobeck, H (1995) An international perspective on practice teaching for foreign students, *Social Work in Europe*, 2 (3), 48–52.

Horner, N (2006) *What is social work? Context and perspectives*. 2nd edition. Exeter: Learning Matters.

Hudson, B, Dearey, M and Glendinning, C (2004) *A new vision for adult social care: scoping service users' views.* Social Policy Research Unit, University of York. York: Department of Health/University of York.

Hughes, G (1998) A suitable case for treatment? Constructions of disability. In Saraga, S (ed.) *Embodying the social: constructions of difference.* London: Routledge.

Hugman, R (1991) *Power and the caring professions*. Basingstoke: Macmillan.

Hugman, R (1998) *Social Welfare and social value*. Basingstoke: Macmillan.

Hugman, R (2005) *New approaches in ethics for the caring professions*. London: Palgrave Macmillan.

Humphries, B (1996) *Critical perspectives on empowerment*. Birmingham: Venture Press.

Humphries, B (2000) Resources for hope: social work and social exclusion. In Batsleer, J and Humphries, B (eds) *Welfare exclusion and political agency*. London: Routledge.

Husen, M (1996) in Pécseli, B *Kultur & pædagogik*. Copenhagen: Munksgaard/Rosinante.

Ife, J (1997) *Rethinking social work: towards critical practice*. Sydney: Longman Pearson.

Ife, J (1999) *Community development: creating community alternatives – vision, analysis and practice.* Sydney: Longman Pearson.

Irish Government (1999) *Equal status bill*. Dublin: Stationery Office.

Johannesen, T (1997) *Social work as an international profession; opportunities and challenges*. In Hokenstad, MC and Midgely, J (eds) *Issues in international social work: global challenges for a new century*. Washington, DC: NASW Press.

Johns, R (2007) *Using the law in social work*. 2nd edition. Exeter: Learning Matters.

Johnson, N, Jenkinson, S, Kendall, I, Bradshaw, Y and Blackmore, M (1998) Regulating for quality in the voluntary sector, *Journal of Social Policy*, 27 (3), 307–28.

Jordan, B (1996) *A theory of poverty and social exclusion*. Cambridge: Polity Press.

Jordan, B (2000) *Social work and the third way: tough love and social policy*. London: SAGE.

Jordan, B (2006) *Social policy for the twenty-first century*. Cambridge: Polity Press.

Joseph Rowntree Foundation (2006) *Findings (0406): The value added by community involvement in governance*. York: Joseph Rowntree Foundation.

Jowitt, M and O'Loughlin, S (2005) *Social work with children and families*. Exeter: Learning Matters.

Kemshall, H (2002) *Risk, social policy and welfare*. Buckingham: Open University Press.

Kendall, J (2000) The mainstreaming of the third sector into public policy in England in the late 1990s: whys and wherefores, *Policy and Politics*, 28 (4), 541–62.

Kendall, KA (2000) *Social work education: its origins in Europe*. Alexandria: Council of Social Work Education.

Langan, M (1998) Radical social work, In Adams, R, Dominelli, L and Payne, M *Social work: themes, issues and critical debates.* Basingstoke: Macmillan.

Langan, M and Lee, P (eds) (1989) *Radical social work today*. London: Unwin Hyman Ltd.

Law Centres Federation (2001) Annual Report *Law centres: putting justice on the social exclusion agenda.* London: Law Centres Federation.

Ledwith, M (1997) *Participating in transformation: towards a working model of community empowerment*. Birmingham: Venture Press.

Levin, E (2004) *Involving service users and carers in social work education*. London: Social Care Institute of Excellence, Resource Guide 2.

Levitas, R (1998) *The inclusive society? Social exclusion and new labour*. Basingstoke: Macmillan.

Lewington, W and Clipson, C (2004) *Advocacy for equality*. London: Independent Advocacy Campaign.

Lister, R (1998) In from the margins: citizenship, inclusion and exclusion. In Barry, M and Hallett, C *Social exclusion and social work – issues of theory, policy and practice*. Lyme Regis: Russell House.

Lord Chancellor's Department and Law Centres Federation, (2001). *Social exclusion*. London: Lord Chancellor's Department.

Lorenz, W (1994) *Social work in a changing Europe*. London: Routledge.

Lorenz, W (1995) Nationalism and racism in Europe: a challenge for pedagogy, *Social Work in Europe*, 2 (3), 34–9.

Lorenz, W (1998) The ECSPRESS approach – the social professions between national and global perspectives, *Social Work in Europe*, 5 (3), 1–8.

Lorenz, W, Aluffi-Pentini, A and Kniephoff, A (1996) Erasmus evaluation: the experience of the social professions; European report. In Seibel, FW and Lorenz, W *Social Professions for a Social Europe, Erasmus Evaluation Conference*, Koblenz, Frankfurt, IKO-Verlag fur Interkulturelle Kommunikation.

Lukes, S (1974) *Power: a radical view*. Basingstoke: Macmillan.

Lymbery, M (2003) Negotiating the contradictions between competence and creativity in social work education, *Journal of Social Work*, 3 (1), 99-117.

Lyons, K (1999) *International social work: themes and perspectives*. Aldershot: Ashgate.

Lyons, K and Lawrence S (2006) *Social work in Europe: educating for change*. Birmingham: Venture Press/BASW.

Lyons, K and Lawrence, S, (2006) Setting the scene: Europe and social work. In Lyons, K and Lawrence, S *Social work in Europe: educating for change.* Birmingham: Venture Press/BASW.

Lyons, M (2006) *Guardian*, October, available at **http://society.guardian.co.uk/futureforpublicservices/story**/ - downloaded 13/11/06).

MacLaughlin, J (1995) *Travellers and Ireland. Undercurrents*. Cork: Cork University Press.

McNay, M (1994) European social work – a degree, *Social Work in Europe*, 1 (2), 15–17.

Maguire, K and Truscott, F (2006) *Active governance: the value added by community involvement in governance in local strategic partnerships*. York: Joseph Rowntree Foundation.

Malin, N, Wilmot, S, Manthorpe, J (2002) *Key Concepts in Health and Social Policy*. Buckingham: Open University Press.

Marynowicz-Hetka, E, Piekarski, J and Wagner, A (1999) Issues in social work: an invitation to a discussion. In Marynowicz-Hetka, E, Wagner, A and Piekarski, J (eds) *European dimensions in training and practice of the social professions*. Katowice: Slask.

Mayo, P (1999) *Gramsci, Freire and adult education*. London: Zed Press.

Melhbye, J (1993) Denmark. In Colton, MJ and Hellinckx, W *Child care in the EC; a country specific guide to foster and residential care*. Aldershot: Arena.

Memmi, A (1990) *The colonizer and the colonized*. London: Earthscan Publications Limited.

Midgely, J (1995) *Social development: the developmental perspective in social welfare*. Thousand Oaks, CA: SAGE.

Midgley, J (1997) *Social work and international social development: promoting a developmental perspective in the profession*. In Hokenstad MC and Midgely, J *Issues in international social work: global challenges for a new century*. Washington, DC: NASW Press.

Miles, S (2007) Different journeys at different speeds: young people, risk and the challenge of creative learning, *Journal of Youth Studies*, 10 (3), 271–84.

MIND (2005) *Factsheet: User empowerment 1 – The user/survivor movement*. London: MIND.

Ministry of Social Affairs (1995a) *Report on the seminar on transfer of know-how and good practice from poverty*. Copenhagen: Ministry of Social Affairs.

Ministry of Social Affairs (1995b) *The good society*. Copenhagen: Ministry of Social Affairs.

Mullaly, R (1997) *Structural social work: ideology, theory and practice*. Toronto: McClelland & Stewart Inc.

Mullard, M and Spicker, P (1998) *Social policy in a changing society*. London, Routledge.

Munday, B (1996) Introduction: definitions and comparisons in European social care. In Munday, B and Ely, P (eds) *Social Care in Europe*. London: Prentice Hall/Harvester Wheatsheaf.

National Anti-Poverty Strategy (1997) *Sharing in progress*. Dublin: Stationery Office.

National Strategic Partnership Forum (2006) *Making partnerships work: examples of good practice*. London: Department of Health.

Nonneman, G, Niblock, T and Szajkowski, B (1997) *Muslim communities in the new Europe*. Reading: Ithaca Press.

North Shields Community Development Project (1974) *Final report*, Volumes 3 and 4.

O'Halloran, C, Hean, S, Humphris, D and Macleod-Clark, J (2006) Developing common learning: the New Generation Project undergraduate curriculum model, *Journal of Interprofessional Care*, 20 (1), 12–28.

Oliver, M (1996) *Understanding disability: from theory to practice*. Basingstoke: Macmillan.

Oliver M and Sapey, B (1999) *Social work with disabled people*. 2nd edition. Basingstoke: Macmillan.

Osborne, SP and McLaughlin, K (2002) Trends and issues in the implementation of local 'Voluntary Sector Compacts' in England, *Public Money and Management: Integrating Research with Policy and*

Practice, January to March, 55–63.

Palmer, G, Carr, J and Kenway, P (2004) *Monitoring poverty and social exclusion 2004*. York: Joseph Rowntree Foundation.

Parker, S, Fook, J and Pease, B (1999) Empowerment: The modernist social work concept *par excellence*. In Pease, B and Fook, J (eds) *Transforming social work practice: postmodern critical perspectives*. London: Routledge.

Parsloe, P (ed.) (1996) *Pathways to Empowerment*. Birmingham: BASW/Venture Press.

PAULO (2002) National Occupational Standards in Community Development Work, **www.fcdl.org.uk/publications/documents/nos/standards**, retrieved 5 July 2006.

Payne, M (1997) *Modern Social Work Theory*. (2nd edition). Basingstoke: Macmillan.

Pease, B and Fook, J (eds) (1999) *Transforming social work practice*. London: Routledge.

Petrie, P (2003) Coming to terms with 'pedagogy': reconceptualising work with children. In Littlechild, B and Lyons, K *Locating the occupational space for social work: international perspectives*. Birmingham: BASW/Venture Press.

Petrie, P (2004) *Briefing paper: Pedagogy – a holistic, personal approach to work with children and young people, across services. European models for practice, training, education and qualification*. London: Thomas Coram Research Unit, Institute of Education, University of London.

Phillips, A (1999) *Which equalities matter*. Cambridge: Polity Press.

Pierson, J (2000) *Tackling social exclusion*. London: Routledge/Community Care.

Pinker, R (1999) – Do poverty definitions matter? In Gordon, D and Spicker, P (eds) *The international glossary on poverty*. London: Zed Books, CROP (Comparative Research Programme on Poverty of the International Social Science Council).

Pinkney, S (1998) Reshaping of social work and social care. In Hughes, G and Lewis, G *Unsettling Welfare: the reconstruction of social policy*. London: Routledge/Open University Press.

Policy Action Team 3 (1999) *National strategy for neighbourhood renewal, enterprise and social exclusion*. London: HM Treasury.

Popple, K (1995) *Analysing community work*. Buckingham: Open University Press.

Popple, K and Redmond, M (2000) Community development in the voluntary sector in the new millennium: the implications of the third way in the UK, *Community Development Journal*, 35 (4), 391–400.

Pridhova, A (1999) Social and legal protection of children and youth in the Czech Republic, *Social Work in Europe*, 6 (3), 38–44.

Pringle, K (1997) Child Protection in England and Wales. In Harder, M and Pringle, K (eds) *Protecting children in Europe: towards a new millenium*. Aalborg: Aalborg University Press.

Pringle, K (1998) *Children and social welfare in Europe*. Buckingham: Open University Press.

Prins, K (2004) *Problem based project work*. Written communication with author.

Quinney, A (2006) *Collaborative social work practice*. Exeter: Learning Matters.

Ramscharan, P, Roberts, G, Grant, G and Borland, J (1997) Citizenship, empowerment and everyday life; ideal and illusion in the new millenium. In Ramscharan, P, Roberts G, Grant, G and Borland, J (eds) *Empowerment in everyday life; learning disability*. London: Jessicca Kingsley.

Rapaport, J, Manthorpe, J, Moriarty, J, Hussein S and Collins, J (2005) Advocacy and people with learning disabilities in the UK: How can local funders find value for money?, *Journal of Intellectual Disabilities*, 9 (94), 299–319.

Revans, L (2001) People with learning difficulties in from the cold, *Community Care*, 29 March–4 April.

Reverda, N (2001) The role of the personal adviser: some observations on social pedagogy from the Netherlands, *Social Work in Europe*, 8 (1), 29–30.

Ritchie, T (2004) *Relationer I teori og praksis.* Copenhagen: Billeso and Baltzer.

Robinson, L (1998) *'Race', communication and the caring professions.* Buckingham: Open University Press.

Rotelli, F, Mezzina, R, De Leonardis, O, Georgen, R and Evaristo, P (n.d.) *Is rehabilitation a social enterprise?* Geneva: Division of Mental Health, World Health Organisation retrieved from **www.triestesalutementale.it/inglese/allegati/rehab.pdf** 20/12/06.

Rowbotham, S, Segal, L and Wainwright, H (1980) *Beyond the fragments: feminism and the making of socialism.* London: Merlin.

Savage, SP and Atkinson, R (eds) (2001) *Public policy under Blair.* Basingstoke: Palgrave.

Schulze, HJ and Wirth, W (1996) *Who cares? social service organizations and their users.* London: Cassell.

Service User Inclusion Group (SUIG) (2005) *Evaluation of Service User Training.* Portsmouth: University of Portsmouth.

Shardlow, S and Payne, M (eds) (1998) *Finding social work in Europe.* In Shardlow, S and Payne, M *Contemporary issues in social work: western Europe.* Aldershot: Arena Ashgate.

Silver, H (1994) Social exclusion and social solidarity: Three paradigms, *International Labour Review*, 1333 (5–6), 531–78.

Simmons, R and Birchall, J (2005) A joined up approach to user participation in public services; strengthening the 'participation chain', *Social Policy and Administration*, 39 (3), 260–83.

Skills for Care (2006) *Learning Resource Network, Review of Progress April 2003 – March 2006.* Leeds: Skills for Care.

Smale, G, Tuson, G and Statham, D (2000) *Social work and social problems: working towards social inclusion and social change.* Basingstoke: Macmillan.

Spear, R (2006) *National profiles of work integration social enterprises: United Kingdom.* Brussels: European Research Network, downloaded from **www.emes.net/fileadmin/emes/PDF_files/ELEXIES** 20/12/06.

Spicker, P (1999) Definitions of poverty: eleven clusters of meaning. In Gordon, D and Spicker, P (eds) (1999) *The international glossary on poverty.* London: Zed Books, CROP (Comparative Research Programme on Poverty of the International Social Science Council).

Stoesz, D and Midgley, J (1991) The radical right and the welfare state. In Glennester, H and Midgley, J *The radical right and the welfare state; an international assessment.* Brighton: Harvester Wheatsheaf.

Tan, H (1998) *Communitarianism: a new agenda for politics and citizenship.* Basingstoke: Macmillan.

Taylor, M (2003) *Public policy in the community.* Basingstoke: Palgrave.

Taylor, Z (1999) Values, theories and methods in social work education: a culturally transferable core?, *International Social Work*, 42 (3), 309–18.

Thompson, J, Alvy, G and Lees, A (2000) Social entrepreneurship – a new look at the people and the potential, *Management Decision*, 38 (5), 328–38.

Thompson, N (1998) *Promoting equality: challenging discrimination and oppression in the human services*. Basingstoke: Macmillan.

Thompson, N (2001) *Anti-discriminatory practice*. Basingstoke: Macmillan.

Thompson, N (2005) *Understanding social work: preparing for practice*. 2nd edition. Basingstoke: Palgrave.

Took, L (2006) *DH social care workforce policy*. Paper presented to the Hants/IOW Learning Resource Network Conference, November 2006.

Toren, N (1969) Semi-professionalism and social work: a theoretical perspective. In Etzioni, A (ed.) *The semi-professions and their organisation; teachers, nurses, social workers*. London: Collier-Mac-millan.

Treseder, P (1995) Involving and empowering children and young people: overcoming the barriers. In Cloke, C and Davies, M *Participation and empowerment in child protection*. London: Pittman Publishing.

Turner, M and Beresford, P (2005) *Contributing on equal terms: service user involvement and the benefits system*. Adult Services Report 08. Bristol: Social Care Institute of Excellence/Policy Press.

Ungerson, C (ed.) (1997) *Women and social policy: a reader*. Basingstoke: Macmillan.

University of Portsmouth (2003) *Making service user involvement effective*. Portsmouth: University of Portsmouth.

Vass, A (1980) The myth of a radical trend in British community work, *Community Development Journal*, 14,1.

Warren, J (2007) *Service user and carer participation in social work*. Exeter: Learning Matters.

Whittington, C (2003) *Learning for collaborative practice with other professions and agencies: A study to inform the development of the degree in social work*. London: Department of Health.

Williams, C, Soydan, H and Johnson, MRD (1998) *Social work and minorities: European perspectives*. London: Routledge.

Williams, F (1999) Balancing polarities: developing a new framework for welfare research. In Williams, F, Popay, J and Oakley, A *Welfare research: a critical review*. London: UCL Press Limited.

Williams, F, Popay, J and Oakley, A (1999) Changing paradigms of welfare. In Williams, F Popay, J and Oakley, A *Welfare research: a critical review*. London: UCL Press Limited.

Williams, GA (1979) *When was Wales?* BBC Wales Annual Radio Lecture, 12 November, Cardiff.

Williams, P (2006) *Social work with people with learning difficulties*. Exeter: Learning Matters.

Wilson, A and Beresford, P (2000) 'Anti-oppressive practice': Emancipation or Appropriation?, *British Journal of Social Work*, 30, 553–73.

Wilson, D (2006) Seduced by the politics of penal populism, *Independent*, 16 August 2006 (**http://comment.independent.co.uk/commentators/article1219467** downloaded 27/03/2007).

Wirth, W and Schulze, HJ (1996) Individual clients in international networks: perspectives of social service integration and user involvement in Europe. In Schulze, HJ and Wirth, W (1996) *Who Cares? Social service organizations and their users*. London: Cassell.

Witz, A (1992) *Professions and patriarchy*. London: Routledge.

Wyatt, M (2002) Partnerships in health and social care: the implications of government guidance in the 1990s in England, with particular reference to voluntary organisations, *Policy and Politics*, 30 (2), 167–82.

Index

Added to a page number 'f' denotes a figure and 't' denotes a table.